THE HEART AND SOUL OF THE TV SOAP OPERA

All
My
Afternoons

by
Annie Gilbert

A & W Visual Library   New York

ORIGINAL PHOTOGRAPHY BY

Mark Sherman

Designed by *Jos. Trautwein*

Grateful acknowledgment is made to the following for permission to use photographs and script material in this book:

PHOTOGRAPHS:

As The World Turns, Guiding Light, Search for Tomorrow and *The Young and the Restless:* Photographs courtesy of the CBS Television Network, a division of Columbia Broadcasting System, Inc.

Another World and *Days of Our Lives:* Photographs courtesy of the National Broadcasting Company.

Mary Hartman, Mary Hartman: Photographs courtesy of T.A.T. Communications Company, copyright © 1976, 1977 by T.A.T. Communications Company.

SCRIPTS:

As The World Turns. Episode 5249/Act I. Copyright © 1976 by Procter & Gamble. Reprinted by permission of Procter & Gamble.

Mary Hartman, Mary Hartman. Episode 43, written by Ann Marcus. Copyright © 1976 by T.A.T. Communications Company. All rights reserved.

Mary Hartman, Mary Hartman. Episode 46, written by Jerry Adelman. Copyright © 1976 by T.A.T. Communications Company. All rights reserved.

Published by
A & W Publishers, Inc.
95 Madison Avenue
New York, New York 10016

Library of Congress Catalog Card Number: 78-70321

ISBN: 0-89104-099-4 (hardcover)
        0-89104-098-6 (paperback)

Printed in the United States of America

ACKNOWLEDGMENTS

In many ways the world of television soap opera is one large, extended family. A great many members of that "family" were of help to me in researching and assembling this book. They ranged from camera technicians to actors, from publicists to producers. I would like to thank all of them collectively, but I would also like to single out a few who were of special assistance: Janet Storm, Phyllis Gardner and Pat Diehl of CBS; Jim Raftery of ABC; Norman Frisch and Leonard Meyers of NBC; Paul Rauch, Mary Bonner, Harding Lemay, Melvin Bernhardt and Victoria Wyndham of *Another World;* Helen Wagner, Don MacLaughlin, Henderson Forsythe and Don Hastings of *As The World Turns;* Charita Bauer of *Guiding Light;* Mary-Ellis Bunim, Robert Getz, Mary Stuart, Larry Haines and Christopher Lowe of *Search for Tomorrow;* Bud Kloss, Mary Fickett and Ruth Warrick of *All My Children;* Wes Kenny, Susan Seaforth Hayes and Bill Hayes of *Days of Our Lives;* John Conboy, Patricia Wenig and Tom Hallick of *The Young and the Restless;* and Norman Lear, Ann Marcus, Al Burton, Virginia Carter, Mary Kay Place and Greg Mullavey of *Mary Hartman, Mary Hartman.*

I would also like to thank Paul Denis of *Daytime TV Magazine,* Geri Jefferson of *Soap Opera Digest,* Milburn Smith of *Afternoon TV Magazine* and Bryna Laub of *Daytime Serial Newsletter.* Anne Kilguss provided information about her work with soap opera therapy groups. Margot Norris contributed an academic perspective on the soaps. Anne Streer told of her experiences as a soap opera fan. Mark Sherman was a dogged and imaginative photographer.

Thank you all.

ANNIE GILBERT

Contents

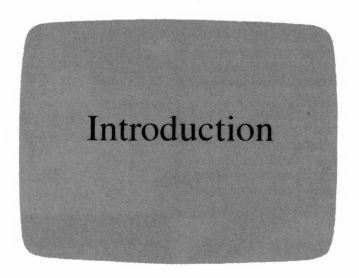

Introduction

SOAP OPERA—good, bad, or indifferent—is part of the private life of fifty million rabidly devoted Americans. On any particular day, from midmorning until late afternoon, five days a week, fifty-two weeks a year, nearly one out of every ten Americans sits in front of a television set and watches life transpire in soap opera towns.

This form of drama goes way beyond entertainment. Beginning in the Depression years and growing up along with America, the stories themselves are like an American history book. They have always reflected their audience, and by offering lessons of life through intricate moral tales of good and evil, they've become something akin to an American Living Bible.

Soaps have generally been considered the deep end not only of the acting profession but of all of television despite the fact that "daytime drama," the colorless euphemism for soap opera, is where television makes its most dependable revenue. None of the networks will reveal the figures, but it's estimated that soaps pull in between 55 and 75 percent of all that the networks earn. Yet they didn't get Emmy Award recognition of any kind until 1972, and it wasn't until 1974 that the daytime Emmy categories were established. They also didn't get scrutinized for content the way nighttime television did, so subjects like abortion, incest, and impotence were the province of the daytime hours long before they were allowed on at night.

Until recently, soaps were also ignored by the press and television critics. Considered "women's entertainment," they were generally not worth paying any attention to unless it was time for a clever, caustic column. Then in 1975 *The New York Times* published an article entitled "Life Can Be Beautiful/Relevent," and soap opera began to come of age.

Over the next several months, other media focused attention on television serials too. Major magazines published features about soaps, including *Ms*, which put out an article in defense of soap watching. Barbara Walters did a story on the *Today* show featuring an NBC soap. Shows like *Upstairs, Downstairs*, while not strictly speaking soap operas, were giving serials a good name with intellectuals. And then word got out that Norman Lear, the man who had fathered *All in the Family* and *Maude*, had created his own comedy soap, and TV critics realized they had better take another look.

It was *Time* magazine that finally gave the soap world what it had been waiting for. In January 1976, *Time* ran a cover story called "Sex and Suffering in the Afternoon." "The ghettoization of the soaps," wrote the *Time* reporters, "has kept them freer of the kind of systematic analysis frequently made of sources of popular culture like comic strips and rock music. . . . " The article gave soap opera its long-sought legitimacy, and suddenly it became a respectable topic of conversation.

In the 1976 presidential election, voters were told of the favorite shows of the candidates' wives and mothers. On college campuses, soap opera was gaining a cult following, with discussions of plotlines replacing discussions of the Vietnam War and R.O.T.C. Kent State, once paralyzed by protests, now had a contented student body that followed the daily doings of Pine Valley folks in *All My Children*. Groups of students sent petitions to soap producers to enlist their help in getting college deans to change course schedules so favorite shows could be followed. And in response to the college fascination with soaps, a number of courses on the subject were introduced, with seminars that study the individual shows and invite stars and writers as guest speakers.

Soaps have a closer and more intimate communication with their audience than any other form of television programming. Since they are intended to mirror ordinary life, their viewers consider themselves experts, with a right and sometimes an obligation to comment on the characters and the direction of the stories. This symbiosis between audience and creators is a very special and important aspect of the soap opera genre.

Each company has its own system for tabulating and using audience mail. One producer acknowledged, "If we get a lot of mail protesting the way the story is going, we'd be foolish not to change it." Paul Rauch, executive producer of *Another World*, says he's happiest when the mail comes in split down the middle on a particular storyline. "If they're involved enough to write in, but 50 percent are in favor and 50 percent are against, then we know we've got something good." Some soap companies also keep track of the number of pieces of mail each actor and actress gets because if a particular character is building up in popularity, they know they improve ratings by expanding that character's storyline.

Another way viewers make their preferences known and so influence the storylines is through the popularity polls run by soap opera fan magazines. Paul Denis, editorial director of *Daytime TV*, explains: "The fans have a lot of power. If they're crazy about somebody and articulate it, the show responds and it affects the story."

Many fans are well aware of their power. One *All My Children* fan wrote in to protest a character getting "killed off." "If you go ahead with it," she wrote, "I'll stop watching the show! Several of my friends feel the same way too!" A very popular actress's fan club president advised her members in their monthly bulletin, "We're not suggesting you should do it, of course, but if you happen to vote twice in the popularity polls, remember to use a different name for each vote." When CBS canceled both *Love Is a Many Splendored Thing* and *Where the Heart Is*, they got over 35,000 letters protesting the decision.

Soaps are big business, meant to sell soap—and dog food and TV dinners and any of thousands of products of particular interest to women. A half-hour show has twenty-two minutes devoted to the storyline and eight minutes for commercials. The cost of each minute, which fluctuates from show to show, is determined by the size of the viewing audience. At one time, for example, a week of *Days of Our Lives* cost approximately $170,000 to produce and brought in approximately $120,000 per day in advertising revenue. According to one source, in fact, *Days* was pulling in $60,000 per advertising minute at the peak of its ratings. Any one of the popular prime-time shows can cost as much or more than that to produce one episode and not bring in half as much in revenue.

Procter & Gamble is the biggest single producer of both soap and soap operas. They got into the soap opera business when they realized that by producing a show themselves they'd control the whole show and get the advertising free. Now P&G own many of the most long-running and top-rated shows—*Search for Tomorrow, The Guiding Light, As the World Turns*, and *Another World* among them.

Though Procter & Gamble Productions own the shows, they do not supervise production directly. Instead, they hire New York advertising agencies and delegate the authority to them to look after production. The agencies hire the producers; the producers in turn are responsible for hiring their staffs and casts. P&G, however, keep a tight rein over the writing of the soap stories themselves.

Robert Short has headed up P&G's soap opera division from the beginning, and he and his staff have become masters at developing and keeping loyal audiences through storyline. They look for what is called a "long-arc" storyline, a story that takes many years to tell. They also take great care to make sure that the storylines they present do not confuse or offend the audience. To this end they have banned proposed stories having to do with subjects ranging from homosexuality to the Vietnam War.

Even Irna Phillips, who ruled the field of soap opera writing for over half a century, had to face their red pencil. When she proposed a storyline about a man who would break up with his wife over another woman and then go off to live with her happily ever after, P&G wouldn't have it. "They told me I could go ahead and let the man divorce his wife," she said of the incident, "but I couldn't let his infidelity be rewarded by having him end up happily married to another woman. It was either keep him around but miserable, or kill him off. I killed him off. He went to Florida, fell over, and hit himself on the head."

As P&G writers, both Harding Lemay and Ann Marcus had proposed plots about homosexuals nixed. "Those meetings were like inquisitions," Marcus said of the regular P&G story conferences. "There'd be the producer of the show, Robert Short and his assistant, and the representative of the advertising agency that was in charge of the show. We'd take up each story I suggested, they'd pull it apart, and I'd have to defend it. They'd say, 'You can't do this,' and I'd yell and scream to try to get them to change their minds. They wouldn't even discuss the homosexual story I tried to get through. They said, 'Forget it, don't waste your breath on it. We're not even going to argue about it.' They said it was too controversial, that it would offend people, and 'We don't want people to turn off their sets or switch to another channel!' The pressure was always to find the storyline that was the least offensive but the most exciting, kind of like a snake, weaving in and out and careful not to offend anyone."

There was a time when soaps were attacked by people who felt they were destroying the minds of American women. One such crusader was psychiatrist Dr. I. Berg, who believed that soap opera watching led to various mental and physical symptoms, from "vertigo and tachycardia to emotional instability." He further believed that widespread soap watching was giving the Axis Powers an edge in World War II by "laying the groundwork for civilian panic in emergencies and sapping the productive energies of the afflicted individuals in all their essential efforts. . . ."

Another person concerned with the psychological impact of soap operas is Anne Kilguss, chief psychiatric social worker at Framingham Union Hospital in Massachusetts, who runs a "soap opera therapy group" at the hospital. She has discovered that discussing soap operas helps women discuss their own personal problems. Kilguss explains her method: "If women watch soap operas, the discussion of such programs can open a path to the patient's unconscious and fantasy life. From the program one works back to the individual and her concerns. This method may be comparable to using play therapy with children. Freud believed that dreams and jokes were the most direct route to the unconscious. I propose that the individual's use and interpretation of the media is another. . . . "

Kilguss feels so many people watch soaps because of "the breakup of the extended family and the isolation that comes as a result of that. Women with very young children living alone with them—children two and three years old—watch soaps to have a peer group, to have company, by watching the lives and listening to the conversations of people their own age—it's like having a circle of friends. And older ladies, alone now, watch to have families they can relate to. You can watch the soaps over a period of years and get to know the people on them better than your own neighbors, and with greater intensity."

From the fans' point of view, soap opera watching can be a very serious business. Most viewers prefer to watch alone because, as one soap writer said, "When they cry, they like to do it privately." After the show is over, viewers compare reactions and predictions. While it might not be considered exactly polite to discuss the personal intricacies of a next-door neighbor's life behind her back, viewers feel not only a clear conscience but even a sense of responsibility about discussing soap opera characters, making adamant judgments about their behavior, and expressing their opinions in writing.

Through stories that spell out lessons, soap operas also give viewers a perspective on their own personal problems and, in a way, provide a guide to living. What will happen if I have an affair with my best friend's husband? What should I do about my stepmother, whom I hate even though I know I'm supposed to be nice to her? Should I sleep with my boyfriend even though we're not married, and what will happen if I turn up pregnant? What will happen if I lie? If I'm too greedy? If I run away from home? If I divorce my husband? If I pursue a career and neglect my children? Soaps answer these and a thousand other questions by meting out punishment to soap characters who do wrong and by lavishing respect and good fortune on those who do right.

There's a lighter side to watching soap opera too, like playing the "soap game," where viewers compare predictions and try to figure out patterns in a particular writer's style. They also follow the careers of soap opera actors as they move from one show to another to TV commercials and back, keeping track of them like baseball players to see who got traded, when, and why. Many soap fans watch their sets with eagle eyes, and if they suspect that one of their favorites is about to be "killed off" and disappear from the show, they'll inundate the production office with letters of protest.

Sometimes viewers forget that it's all make-believe. A college professor who follows *The Young and the Restless* said, "I didn't realize how caught up I was until they changed an actor who was playing one of the parts. It shocked me into remembering that the whole thing isn't real." Viewers also write letters addressed not to actors but to the characters themselves, expecting intimate replies as if they'd written to a close friend. "Most of the time they don't know our real names," a soap actor said with chagrin. In fact, according to one soap director, "There are people out there—not lots of them, but a certain proportion—who think this is documentary television. They think we've really got a camera set up in someone's living room."

At the core of every soap opera there's the family, and some stretch out to three and four generations. There are the grandparents the young folks seek out for advice; their children, who can't seem to make their marriages work the way their parents did; the grandchildren, who as the children of divorce suffer from lack of family stability. There are sisters who squabble over boyfriends, brothers who compete, parents who disapprove of their children's choice of mates.

Soaps have grown up economically right along with the American public. The first soap characters were tradesmen and carpenters from poor and immigrant families. Gradually they became lawyers and doctors, professions which are the very symbols of what it meant to aspire to status in America. Now many soap characters are upper middle class; they own large businesses and their children have become writers and artists. Most soap families are trying to get ahead, but the underlying theme is always there: too much ambition brings ruination.

Though soaps are supposed to reflect ordinary life, they often seem anything but ordinary because of the human suffering, disease, death, and divorce that are an endless plague on their families. One reason for this is that a soap has a limited number of characters, and they have to be used over and over again in storylines. Taken one by one, the situations aren't unreal, but the way they mount up on one person or family makes it all seem ridiculous. Another inescapable soap problem is that due to limitations of time and money, soap stories generally take place indoors on a limited number of sets. This means that soap characters tend to talk about what they did rather than actually do it.

Though the networks insist that more men than ever are watching soap operas, daytime TV is primarily meant for women. That fact makes the place of women in the soap stories even more interesting. On the one hand, soaps have some of the only complex roles for women in television; on the other, the stories themselves generally reinforce the belief that a woman's ultimate job in life is to take care of her family and stay at home. Soaps have lots of professional women characters—from doctors and psychiatrists to newspaper reporters—but single successful women are inevitably neurotic, and most, whenever given the opportunity, put their love affairs above their work. The ultimate soap woman seems to be the one who proves her strength by knowing how to suffer in silence.

Soap opera is the most persistent dramatic form to have found its way to television. And it seems destined, despite its stepchild status, to keep its place in the hearts and minds of its fifty million viewers. Those make-believe people who come to life for a half hour or hour each day have a most uncanny way of becoming real. The Hughes family of Oakdale, the Brooks of Genoa City, the Matthews of Bay City—are all likely to keep turning out new generations for years.

Irna Phillips.

*Irna Phillips
and the Origins of
Soap Opera*

A RADIO ANNOUNCER named Norman Brokenshire claims to have discovered soap opera by accident. One afternoon when the actors he had hired didn't show up, he spotted a book lying open on the desk in front of him and began to read to his listening audience. He was halfway through one story when the recalcitrant actors appeared, so Brokenshire put the book aside. The next week stacks of letters arrived at the station asking about the fate of the characters in the story he had begun. Brokenshire obliged by finishing up the story on the air, and radio soaps were born.

The antecedent of soap opera was the nineteenth-century novel. Struggling writers such as Charles Dickens, Henry James, and Anthony Trollope were paid by the word to produce stories that were serialized in weekly or monthly installments. Their device of weaving in a reminder of past events is similar to the recapitulation device used by soap opera writers today.

But *The Amos and Andy Show* is really where it all began. Freeman Gosden and Charles Correll created the famous radio duo in 1929, and they both wrote the scripts and read the parts on the air. Soon their show became a national craze. So many Americans followed the endless predicaments of these two hapless characters that the phone company reported a drop in use each evening while the show was on the air. The secret to their success, and what later became the crucial ingredient in soap operas too, was that they created characters people cared about; the stories were not as crucial as the ultimate fate of Amos and Andy.

Pepsodent toothpaste sponsored the show, and

The days of radio soaps: Right to Happiness, *1944.*

when other advertisers saw sales of the product soar, they started scouting around to see if they could get into the radio story business too.

At first the stories were on the air only at night; the daytime radio waves were still a bleak desert of cattle reports, advice on hygiene, and instructions on growing vegetables. But the story shows were so successful, advertisers began to consider airing them during the day for the housewife audience. Soon the first daytime radio serial went on the air. It was sponsored by a sausage factory.

By the time an Ohio schoolteacher named Irna Phillips arrived in Chicago to try to launch a career as a radio actress, the radio storytelling business was about to blossom into a full-scale multimillion-dollar entertainment form. Irna Phillips had grown up in Chicago one of ten children, graduated with an M.A. in drama from the University of Illinois (which at the time was no ordinary accomplishment for a woman), and then had gone to work in Dayton, Ohio, teaching storytelling and children's drama. When she decided to audition for an acting part at Chicago radio station WGN, her luck turned out to be mixed. "The station manager told me my voice was not pleasant, that it

was too low for a woman," Phillips remembered. However, so the legend goes, he did sign her up to read a daily program called *Thought for a Day*. She was twenty-eight, and that was enough incentive for her to quit her teaching position and move back to Chicago. A few weeks later, she lost the job. But then the station manager asked her if she'd try writing and performing a continuing family story to run for ten minutes a day.

Her first serial, *Painted Dreams*, went on the air in 1932. The main character was Mother Moynihan, an Irish mother of a large family and a woman Irna apparently modeled closely after her own mother. Mother Moynihan's continued sage advice expressed the theme that came to underscore all of Irna Phillips's later stories: " . . . I'm thinking that a country is only as strong as its weakest home. When you're after destroyin' those things which make up a home, you're destroyin' people. . . . " This idea of families surviving the challenges and troubles of daily life was the foundation on which the young writer created the new genre "soap opera."

Painted Dreams was written by Irna and a partner who divided up the characters and read them on the air. She took two; her partner took four plus the dog. A dispute over who owned the rights to the show developed when Irna wanted to sell the show to a network for national airing. WGN said it was theirs; she said it was hers. So Irna took her characters, gave them new names, put them in another town, and continued writing the same serial for NBC.

Soaps were now a nationally syndicated business. Irna no longer had time to act the parts on the air; she had all she could do to turn out the scripts for an ever-increasing number of shows—*Today's Children, The Guiding Light, Woman in White, Right to Happiness*, and the many others that quickly followed. Soon the airwaves were humming throughout the day with intimate stories of family travails. Radio stations in Chicago were crowded with actors hurrying to assigned air times as stagehands worked in the background making doorbells ring, cars start, trains crash. According to soap opera legend, there were times when Irna was so busy she'd be seated at a table at one side of the studio writing the dialogue seconds before the actors said the lines on the air.

The pioneering radio soaps were clichéd and melodramatic. *Our Gal Sunday* opened each new episode with that classic intonation: "This is the story that asks the question—can a girl from a little mining town in Colorado find happiness with the rich and titled Lord Henry Brinthrop?" Religion had center stage in these early serials, but it was a homespun American variety that emphasized family loyalty, neighborly forgiveness, and a straightforward morality that stuck close to the Ten Commandments. Soap characters who sinned, were selfish, thoughtless, or greedy inevitably got in trouble; characters who were good and upstanding got respect and a happy life. Parents always played a central part. They were dispensers of family wisdom, and they worried endlessly about the unhappy fates of their children.

At the height of her career Irna Phillips was reportedly turning out 60,000 words a week, the length of a fair-sized novel. Those three million words a year earned her a quarter of a million dollars annually. "I dictate all my scripts," she once explained. "That allows me to play the parts of all my characters and give them dialogue that sounds like real, colloquial speech. And I avoid tape recorders. I dictate to another person to get that essential human contact, that other person's reaction to my dialogue, that raised eyebrow that tells me a word or a phrase doesn't sound right. . . ."

Until her death in 1973, Irna Phillips was acknowledged as the reigning queen of soaps. She was not the first serial writer to parlay the new genre into a successful business, however. The husband and wife team of Anne and Frank Hummert began work in 1933, set up a soap story factory in their home in Greenwich, Connecticut, and earned as much as a million dollars a year writing many of the radio soaps that became daytime staples—*Our Gal Sunday, Backstage Wife*, and *Just Plain Bill* among their most popular. The Hummerts ran their script-writing

organization with an iron rule, overseeing a collection of assistant writers who mass-produced scripts, paying low wages, and firing anybody who tampered with their prescriptions for storylines. Anne Hummert apparently once declared to a writer, "I want to see God on every page!"

By the mid-forties soap operas were big business. In the early radio soap days, sponsors had been content to have the names of their products woven subtly into the storylines—the heroine would serve the sponsor's soup for lunch or wash the dinner dishes with the sponsor's dishwashing product. Then Proctor & Gamble introduced frenzy into radio selling by offering prizes in boxtop contests. Gradually, with the introduction of regular commercial breaks, advertising became more sophisticated and advertisers began to take more care to be sure their products were well presented. When soap writer Elaine Carrington created a show to be called "Red Adams" and Beech-Nut Gum decided to sponsor it, for example, they insisted she change the name of her character. Adams Gum, after all, belonged to Beech-Nut's competition, and so young Red Adams became Red Davis.

When television began to gain popularity and there was talk of trying out soaps in the new visual form, most people considered the idea ridiculous. Producing a radio soap cost about $3500 a week; with the need for costumes, props, and sets, a television soap could easily cost two to three times as much. Also, there was doubt that TV soaps could gain an audience. The radio soaps were supposed to be listened to by women as they went about their work in the home; how many would be willing to take time out from the work they had to get done to sit down in front of the set?

The first television soap opera began on CBS in 1950, and it quickly proved to be a flop. Entitled *The First Hundred Years*, it was meant to tell the story of the first hundred years of a marriage. It never saw the last ninety-nine. Other TV soaps also tried and failed, but finally, under the guidance of a man named Roy Winsor, whose luck with TV soap operas earned him the title of CBS's "father soap," television serials began to take hold. Shows like *The Guiding Light* and *Young Doctor Malone*, which began on radio, were now presented in television versions. At the same time, network television was growing fast and beginning to pose a threat to radio. In an effort to fight back, many radio stations turned away from nationally syndicated programing, doing local shows of their own to attract local sponsors. Since soaps were among those programs distributed through the networks, they now started to disappear from the air. By the late 1950's only a few were left, and on Thanksgiving Day 1960, the very last radio soap wound up its final story.

In the late thirties and forties soap opera had begun to move out of Chicago to New York, and by the time television soaps took hold, they were firmly based in New York City. With her dominance in the field, Irna Phillips was able to stay put in Chicago and mail her scripts to the producers, making her presence felt by infrequent trips to New York and constant telephone calls. By this time she had earned a reputation for being nearly dictatorial in her commandments about characters and actors. When she met the actors, she would almost always address them by their character names, and those who did not please her, for any of a number of reasons, found themselves out of work.

Meanwhile, soaps were growing in length. They had gradually expanded to fifteen minutes on radio, and the fifteen-minute episode was carried over to TV. Next Irna Phillips pressed to double the time. She believed that in a half-hour format there would be more room for character development and more time to portray feelings, emotions, and characters' reactions visually.

Initially the networks balked at the idea of the longer format. It took a tenacious fight before Irna got her way. Though they didn't allow her to expand any of the existing shows to a half hour, they agreed she could write a new one. She wrote *As the World Turns*, which became CBS's most successful, dependable, and highest-rated soap. With the creation of *As the World Turns* and the half-hour format, a new era of TV soap operas—richer, more complex and dramatic—was born.

In many ways, the history of soap opera is the history of Irna Phillips. For example, the soapy trick of giving a character amnesia whenever a quick switch in plotline was in order was an Irna Phillips invention. The preponderance of medical problems and strange diseases was also her doing. Unusually preoccupied with matters of her own personal health, she kept a shelf of medical books to consult both to look up her own ailments and to research the details and symptoms of the diseases she gave to her characters. She also consulted regularly with quite a few doctors. In addition to talking with them about her own medical problems, she'd pump them for information. She'd tell them, "I need to lose a character for four weeks. What kind of disease can I use?" Her doctors would comply with suggestions.

To this day the soap opera field is dominated by writers Irna Phillips trained and influenced. The two most highly acclaimed soap writers currently in the business, Agnes Nixon and William Bell, apprenticed with her. Both started as script writers, eventually became headwriters, and then became creators of their own shows. Both carry on the tradition she began of writing soaps that emphasize family life.

Irna Phillips was outspoken about her own philosophy and insistent until her death that the morality presented through the soap opera form be carefully preserved. She once commented, "I have never had a serial canceled, and every serial I created has a family at the center. I have tried to show the American public that I believe in Americanism and the home. The family is the greatest influence we have, and it can return to being part of our lifestyle."

Ironically, Irna Phillips never married even though she did eventually adopt two children. Yet she gave birth to more characters and kept more actors thriving and at work than perhaps anyone else since Shakespeare. She created a dramatic form, she established a tradition, she worked nearly fifty years at her trade, and when she was done, Irna had written in words and stories the equivalent of 2500 novels.

Confessions of a Soap Opera Fan

ANNE STREER, twenty-eight years old, has watched "the stories" since she was a young girl. Her earliest fantasy was to go to New York and be an actress on *Search for Tomorrow*. Instead she went to college at the University of Indiana and then moved to Los Angeles, where she now works in the music business. Below she follows her passion from its earliest days.

I started watching soaps as soon as we got our first TV—1954 or 1955. I was heavy into the CBS soaps. All day. *Love of Life* was on at ten-thirty, then *Search for Tomorrow, Guiding Light, As the World Turns, The Edge of Night, Secret Storm*. I'd watch with my mother; she was really into it then. No matter what kind of mood she was in, she'd sit and watch. On one of those days when all the kids were being crazy, she'd be screaming . . . but by the time one of her favorites, like *As The World Turns*, was over with, she was pretty well mellowed out. It was like therapy for her. I was thinking the other day how when I'm

"You can learn a lot by watching soap operas. I saw my first French kiss on a soap."

sick and the soaps are on, it's security for me. A vacuum cleaner running and a soap opera on the television . . . I guess it will always have that calming effect.

I grew up in South Bend, Indiana. We were middle class. Soap operas make you conscious of things like that, of class. Each soap has a rich family in the town, and the story might be something along the lines of a Romeo and Juliet thing with a rich old lady's son wanting to marry a girl who is just a secretary and comes from a poor family. They'd build a whole plot around how the rich mother tries to stop her precious son from being involved with this girl.

One story I'll always remember was when Sarah Carr died on *Edge of Night*. It was the story that affected me the most of all. Her daughter Laurie Anne had just had an operation and come home from the hospital. Someone had left the front door open and little Laurie Anne had wandered out into the street. When Sarah saw a car coming toward her in the road, she ran out into the street to save her. All you heard was the sound of screeching brakes and horns blowing and Sarah screaming. That was Friday. We had to go through the whole weekend worrying about it. When Monday came around, the family was right in front of the set. It turned out that Sarah had pushed little Laurie to safety, but she'd gotten hit herself, and a couple of days later she died. It was probably my first real contact with death. At that point in my life, no one close to me had ever died. I was nine, I think. I was supposed to go over a friend's house, and I remember being in a daze all the way there and crying. That's how involved I'd get.

At one point I was so involved in soap operas all I wanted to do was be an actress. As far back as I can remember I wanted to move to New York City, live in some walk-up apartment, and be on the Joanne Tate show. I wanted to be somebody's daughter or girlfriend or something.

Joanne Tate (played by Mary Stuart on *Search for Tomorrow*) was so steadfast. I don't remember her ever raising her voice. I remember thinking how could she be on television all the time when she's not even that pretty? It was like women's lib, you know. She was the main character, and although she was not gorgeous, she was so good and so smart that everybody went to her. She was very maternal. The people who watch, they're like her children. It's like we grew up together. I knew her before I knew some of my relatives. I knew her better than I knew my friends. I was conscious of a lot of these soap opera people before I was really conscious of most people in the real world.

Now that I work all I can really see is *Love of Life*. It's on at ten-thirty, and I don't have to be at work until eleven. I leave the minute the music starts playing at the end.

You can learn a lot by watching soap operas. I saw my first French kiss on a soap. Generally I think soaps have shown me what not to do with my life—like not getting involved in extra-marital affairs. From all the stories I've watched on soaps I can see that it leads to no good. When a married man went out with some woman, you just knew something bad was going to happen. Somebody would get killed or somebody would have a nervous breakdown. Sometimes now when I have friends going through strange situations with husbands or girlfriends or whatever, I'll flash back to a similar situation I remember from some soap opera. If I try, I can usually think of some show in the last ten or fifteen years with a plot that would be similar to the kind of situation I'm seeing.

It's the same with Mary Hartman. Mary Hartman was the epitome of everything negative that ever happens to anybody on a soap opera. People identified with her. She really tried to be good to everybody, and then she got kicked in the ass. Mary Hartman showed the general confusion that so many people feel these days. There are a lot of Mary Hartmans running around. That show did a lot for people. People are aware that they're nuts and they'd say, "Oh, I feel like Mary Hartman today." I've said it many times myself. Mary Hartman was like a warm Teddy bear. You could hang on to it and go to sleep at night.

GUIDING LIGHT

THE GUIDING LIGHT isn't just soap opera, it's American history. Three generations of Bauers have descended from Papa Bauer, an immigrant carpenter. His grandsons, Michael and Ed, both fulfilled the American dream by becoming successful professionals. This is a soap opera that celebrates the American ideal: If you work hard, save your money, and stick close to family and home, you'll not only be happier for it, but good fortune will come your way.

The Guiding Light is the only serial originating on radio that is still going strong on television. It began in 1937 as one of Irna Phillips's early creations, and it

Charita Bauer played Bert Bauer and Lyle Sudrow played her husband, Bill, in the early television years of the Guiding Light. *Charita still plays Bert Bauer to this day.*

soon shared the airwaves with some seventy-three other serials. It made the transition to television in 1952, and for four years the radio and television versions ran simultaneously. Most actors played the same parts on both, spending their mornings rehearsing and performing the day's script for live TV, then hurrying across town to stand in front of microphones and read the radio version in the afternoon. In 1968 *Guiding Light* expanded from its fifteen-minute format to a half hour. In 1977, the year the show celebrated forty years of continuous broadcasting and became the oldest daytime serial in the world, it expanded to an hour.

The Guiding Light actually had two entirely different incarnations, changing not only characters and locale in midstream, but also its dominant story. In the original radio version it had a purely inspirational

Fans of the Guiding Light *sent in greetings for Papa Bauer's (played by* Theo Goetz) *sixty-fifth birthday.*

theme consistent with its title. The "guiding light" was meant to help people through a period of American history when poverty and war had undermined the nation's spirit. Stories revolved around the lives of Reverend Rutledge's parish. Problems would test the parishioners' faith, but the Reverend's guidance would see them through. The underlying theme was that faith brings happiness, and sometimes a whole episode would be devoted to a sermon from the pastor to drive the point home.

When radio serials began to outgrow the Windy City, *The Guiding Light* moved with the rest of them to New York, where the original story was revamped. In the 1940's the Bauer family was born, and Reverend Rutledge dropped out of the picture.

The story's locale changed from Five Points to Selby Flats and eventually to the city of Springfield, where small-town life was left behind for the pressures and challenges of the city.

The old inspirational theme persisted through this change, but Reverend Rutledge's spiritual lessons were now woven into the fabric of family life. Instead of challenges to religious faith, the story told of threats to the stability and perseverance of family and home. Romance, insanity, disease, and even murder tested the strength of the Bauers. Each time they triumphed it proved that a family of good will could stay together.

The clan got its start in America when Papa and Mama Bauer arrived from Europe to settle in

California. They had three children—Bill, Meta, and Trudy. Shortly after Bill married Bert, Mama Bauer passed away and the family regrouped around Bill and Bert, with Papa maintaining his position as the dispenser of wisdom and advice.

The marriage between Bert and Bill had problems that typified struggling Americans. Bill, like his father before him, believed in the value of hard work and was firmly committed to the precept that earned income should precede frivolous spending. But Bert wanted a home, and she nagged at her husband for it. When he wouldn't give in, she went out and put a down payment on a house behind his back. Eventually the strains of work, family pressures, and an illicit love affair drove Bill to drink. With the support of his family, he battled against alcoholism and eventually stopped drinking. Later his son Ed, a surgeon at Cedars Hospital, followed in his footsteps—twice. The first time he hook to drinking, he also took to beating up his wife, Leslie. Eventually the two of them got divorced, but in the meantime Ed's brother, Michael, a lawyer, had begun to fall in love with Leslie. The two kept their affection a secret until the divorce was final, but then Leslie had a child by Ed, which made Mike turn to another woman. Finally, Mike and Leslie got together again and were married.

Over the years Bert became the pillar of family strength. When her husband supposedly died in a plane crash (he was "resurected" ten years later and brought back into the story for a while), she assumed leadership of the Bauer clan. Papa Bauer remained the family arbiter of wisdom, and he and Bert were very close, but she held the day-to-day family life together. She still does. Even as the Bauers move into their fourth generation in America (and on the air), the family rallies around Grandma Bert whenever there are troubles to face.

At one time the Bauers moved over to another serial on another network. Michael, distraught over the suicide of his first wife, left Springfield with his daughter to start a new life. They arrived in Bay City, hometown of the NBC serial *Another World*, in time to help an ailing John Randolph with his law practice. But when Mike fell in love with John's wife, it was time to get him out of Bay City. Writer Irna Phillips, who had engineered the initial move (she wrote both shows at the time), wrote him out of *Another World* and back into *Guiding Light*.

Mart Hulswit currently plays Ed Bauer, and it was in a moment of soap opera philosophizing that he dubbed the *Guiding Light* theme "Bauer Power." In fact, this phenomenon of "Bauer Power" has had its impact both on screen and off. Completely by coincidence, Bert Bauer has been played on TV from the beginning by an actress with the same last name. It's no coincidence that her real-life son and television son are both named Michael. Charita Bauer did this to avoid unnecessary confusion in keeping her on-screen and off-screen sons' names straight.

Both in front of the camera and behind it, Charita Bauer is matriarch of a persevering family clan. The people who produce *The Guiding Light*—actors and actresses as well as directors, technicians, and stagehands—have developed into a close-knit group over the years. For example, Lynne Adams, who played Leslie Bauer, was the second generation of her family to appear on the show; both her parents had acted in the radio version.

Theo Goetz, the actor who played Papa Bauer from the origin of the character until his own death, was the truest example and embodiment of this phenomenon of "Bauer Power." Goetz basically played himself in the part and used the role to expound softly on his beliefs on how people and families should treat one another.

Goetz himself was an immigrant to America. In the story, Papa Bauer had come from Germany; in real life, Goetz fled Austria. With Hitler's rise to power, Goetz decided to leave his homeland, a highly successful career as a stage actor, and all his possessions behind. When he arrived in America he had no friends, no family, no place to go, and nothing but the equivalent of two dollars in his pocket. Since he couldn't speak English, he adopted the neighborhood movie theater as his home and English teacher.

"People have no idea what goes into writing these soaps. It's planned like the most complicated military strategy. You need a storyline for Liza or Steve, and you have to resolve the euthanasia murder and figure out who did it and tie it up, and there's a trial and you have to figure out the outcome of that too. It's like a chess game with various different elements all going on at the same time."

—a soap opera writer

"It's kind of a sandwich, whose recipe is simple enough, although it took years to compound. Between thick slices of advertising, spread about twelve minutes of dialogue, add predicament, villainy, and female suffering in equal measure, throw in a dash of nobility, sprinkle with tears, season with organ music, cover with a rich announcer sauce, and serve five times a week."

—James Thurber's definition of soap opera

As soon as he felt he had learned enough of the new language, he made the rounds of casting offices. The first part he landed was a doctor on the radio soap *Young Doctor Malone*. Then in 1949 he auditioned before the obstreperous Irna Phillips, and she picked him for the new part she was creating on *Guiding Light* of an old-country immigrant father.

Goetz and Papa shared more than a stage personna. Goetz was often heard to remark, "God wanted me to play Papa Bauer," and most people believe he basically played himself, affirming the value of the same tenaciousness that had helped him survive in America. He preached love, tolerance, and kindness, and when Papa celebrated his sixty-fifth birthday in the story, over 39,000 letters of congratulations arrived for him at the studio. Goetz, a modest and unassuming man, was quite moved when he saw the piles of mail and said, "I get so many loving letters. I think Papa fills a great need. Here there is a father, an old European kind of father, who is a worry wart, who loves his family. Many of the audience don't know what it could be, a love between father and children. . . ."

When Goetz died at the age of seventy-seven, there was no effort to try to replace him in the part; Papa Bauer's own death was simply written into the story. Mart Hulswit, in his part as Papa's grandson, gave the on-screen eulogy: " . . . when he was young he loved his native land, but soon some terrible things began to happen there. And so he found his way to this country. And a passionate love for this his adopted country began to grow in him. He made it his country, its history, his history. He would never let us call him a wise man. He would only say that if you live a long time, you live through so much that you begin to have an understanding of human events. . . ." Hulswit was certainly speaking about both the actor and the character, but he was also summing up the attitude and morality of *The Guiding Light*'s abiding theme, illustrated in an endless saga of love, marriage, infidelity, and divorce while the Bauers keep hammering home the conviction that family solidarity brings happiness.

Charita/Bert Bauer's Photo Album

Charita Bauer played Bert Bauer on the Guiding Light from its first days on television. As such, she has earned the position of cast mother, cast historian, and "the guiding light." Here she takes a look at an album of photographs that depicts some of the history of the show and shares her memories of those years gone by.

"This is from the very beginning of the show when we first went on television. From left to right, there's Ted Corday, Lucy Rittenberg, David Lesan, and the representative of the advertising company that looked after us. Lucy has just recently retired, but she knew the show from the very beginning. She started as an assistant to the director and ended up as an executive producer. David Lesan was the show's original producer, and he's the man who hired me. Ted Corday was the show's first director on television. He was a wonderful man. After three or four years with us he went with Irna Phillips to work on As the World Turns. *After that he went on to create* Days of Our Lives. *When things weren't working out on the floor, he'd push the talk-back button and say, 'I'm coming out.' It became a standard joke because the technicians would say, 'Head for the hills, he's coming out!' He had so many memorable sayings that eventually the crew got together and wrote them all up on a big cardboard and numbered them. 'I'm coming out' became number six. After that if he'd push the talk-back button to say he was coming out, we just referred to it as 'number six.'*

"That's me as Bert with Theo Goetz, who played my father-in-law, Papa Bauer. I was married to Papa's son Bill. This is about twenty years ago, right after we first went on television. When we first went on TV we thought that it was going to be wonderful, that we would have the freedom of not being tied to the microphone all the time and be able to invest the action with new life. But that hope was quickly scotched. The potential of these shows has never been touched—and I mean all of them, not just ours. I don't mean to be putting the soaps down. I think some wonderful things have come out. But think of the opportunity of a drama that goes on and on. What could have become a minor art form was nipped in the bud in the ___nning. It's an essentially commercial medium. I don't mean that because it's commercial it couldn't be creative. I don't believe those two things are mutually exclusive. But it all got formularized early on. It became a set piece and the forest was lost sight of for the trees."

"That's Lyle Sudrow, who played Bill Bauer, Papa's son and my husband. That's Glen Walken, who played our son Michael. In the early days Bert tended to be a bit manipulative. She would try to twist her husband around her finger, and Bill would get impatient. When she was much younger and when they were first married she used to do all sorts of crazy things—like putting money down on a house without telling her husband and going off and buying herself a mink stole. But that was all on radio. By the time she got to television, she had begun to settle down."

"This is me with my sister-in-law Meta, who was played by Ellen Demming. She was on the show for fourteen years. In the early days on radio Meta was one of the Bauer children who really kicked up her heels, leaving home and going off to have a big romance and a baby out of wedlock. Gradually over the years, she mellowed, and she became a more conventionally stable character. When she first played the part, like most of us, Ellen was really too young for the character. We were all in our twenties when we first started, and Ellen as Meta was supposed to be around thirty-five. Ted Corday decided to have her wear a bun to make her look older and had little white bits of hair glued to her temples. They never really looked like anything but clumps of white hair, and we called them her 'little gray wings.' Back then we smoked on television. Even though my character was a wife and mother and basically a good character, she was allowed to smoke. Now no one smokes. Since the Surgeon General's report on the dangers of smoking, the Procter & Gamble shows don't allow people to smoke."

"Tension developed between Bill and I when Bill went off and got involved with a nightclub singer named Gloria. She was beautiful and glamorous, and soon he was having a fling with her while I was busy with my second baby. Here, Papa and Bill are arguing, and probably Bill is complaining to his father about me. They didn't argue often because Bill was a very good son and Papa was usually understanding and tolerant. But he didn't approve of the thing with Gloria, and here he's letting his son know it."

"Later on in the story, Meta started going out with a man named Mark Holden, played by Whit Conner. At the center of the picture there's Robin, Meta's step-granddaughter. Robin was played by Zina Bethune and she had a theme song they used to play on the organ: 'Poor little Robin—walk, walk, walkin' to Missouri . . . can't afford to fly . . .'"

"Here, Mark Holden and my husband, Bill, are talking over Mark's problems in love. By now he's discovered that he doesn't love Meta, Bill's sister, but loves her stepdaughter Kathy instead, and probably Bill is trying to offer some consolation."

"Kathy and Mark are explaining to Robin that they plan to get married. Robin got very upset and tried to stop the marriage."

"Here's Ellen playing Meta again. She's with Bruce Banning, who became her third husband. When the two of them got married there was a problem because Les Damon, who played the part of Bruce at that time, was shorter than Ellen. They had a scene on Observatory Hill when he was proposing marriage, but since she was taller than him she had to do the whole scene in her stocking feet. It was a big romantic scene, and though you couldn't see it on the screen, there she was with no shoes on."

"Papa is wishing Ellen well in her new life with Bruce. Papa always had that role. He was the pater familias. You had to get his blessing. He was always very kind and loving and not a butinsky."

"Left to right, there's Dick Grant played by Jimmy Lipton, Marie played by Lynn Rogers, and Dr. Paul Fletcher played by Bernie Grant. Dick and Marie were married and Marie was always very big on making spaghetti. Meta, my sister-in-law, was very big on serving tomato juice and chocolate buds. No one ever figured out what chocolate buds were. I think they were candy kisses, but I don't know. Maybe they're something they had in Chicago, where the writer, Irna Phillips, lived."

"And here are Robin and Peggy. That's Frannie Myers (right) as a young girl. She's grown up and still plays on the show today. We're dressing-roommates, and she and I have become great friends. She's one of the really close friends I've made in the world, even though she's younger than my own son. When an actor named Roger Newman came on the show to play the part of Ken Norris, he and Fran fell in love. Now they've gotten married and they have a little baby."

"Maggie Scott is talking with her estranged husband, who was played by Bernard Kates. Maggie was another woman who got involved with my husband, Bill. They worked together, had an affair, and fell very much in love. The Scotts had had a child, Peggy, who was played by Fran Myers. When her parents were both killed, Peggy came to stay with me for a while."

"Dr. Paul Fletcher was a wonderful man and a very fine doctor, truly devoted to medicine. He opened a clinic for the poor, and this caused problems between him and his wife, Anne who came from a well-to-do family and did not particularly enjoy the kind of life Paul wanted to lead. It wasn't that she was such a terrible snob, it was just that she was brought up differently. A great deal of difficulty arose between them as a result. And when Paul hired an ex-alcoholic to help him in the clinic, it was just too much for Anne to take. This woman started drinking again and by accident struggled with Anne over a gun. The gun went off, Anne got killed, and Paul had to go on trial for the murder. Eventually he got acquitted, and later married Robin. The nurse in the picture is Paul's sister, played by Chase Crowsley."

"This is Ed Bryce, the actor who replaced Lyle Sudrow in the part of Bill. Here we are having coffee in the kitchen. It's some time in the early sixties. It was when he was still having troubles with drinking."

"This is Lynne Adams, who played Leslie, with Bob Gentry, who at that time played Dr. Ed Bauer. This was taken in the mid-sixties. They're quarreling here, but eventually the two of them got married. They had a child and then they ended up divorced."

"These are my two grown sons, Ed and Michael. Ed is played by Mart Hulswit and Michael is played by Don Stewart. They have had a good relationship as brothers except for the time that one ended up marrying the other's ex-wife. They wouldn't have had a storyline like that in the old days; a story like that breaks down family ties. Now they don't really care about the idea of the family anymore. That used to be the main theme of the show, but now it's gone."

Search for Tomorrow

SEARCH FOR TOMORROW is a soap aptly named—for over twenty-seven years it's been Joanne Barron Tate Reynolds Vincente's search for some abiding personal happiness, to say nothing of a husband who won't go crazy, die of a heart attack, become alcoholic, get shot to death, or in some other way let her down. It was the creation of Roy Winsor, who gave many of CBS's soaps their start, and what he had in mind was a modern version of *Stella Dallas* or *The Romance of Helen Trent,* both radio soap classics featuring a woman as the strong central character. Joanne Tate, star character of *Search for Tomorrow,* was meant to be an exemplary woman with whom millions of American women could iden-

John Wyatt (Val Dufour) *and wife Eunice* (Ann Williams). *All went well between them until John met the young, beautiful, and troublesome Jennifer Pace. She killed Eunice when John broke up their affair to return to his marriage.*

tify as they followed her through her struggles, her loneliness, her triumphs. Winsor saw Joanne as a kind of young Ma Perkins, ''the sort of woman who cared about her neighbor's problems, who would offer help to others, and who could face her own personal troubles with dignity.'' She was to be a young widow bringing up a daughter on her own, never allowed for long to depend on the support of a stable marriage.

Search for Tomorrow, the longest-running TV serial on the air, started in 1951 as a fifteen-minute black-and-white segment that cost $8073 per week to produce. Now it's done in color, it's a half hour, and the cost for production has gone up to $110,000 a week. Henderson, the home of *Search,* has been around as long as many incorporated towns, and if *Search*'s producer, Mary-Ellis Bunim, who worked her way up from production assistant over twelve

(L to r) Keith Barron (John Sylvester), *Patti Barron* (Lynne Loring), *and
Joanne Barron* (Mary Stuart). *Keith was Joanne's first husband. He died
early in their marriage in a car accident.*

years, could be considered the town mayor, Mary
Stuart, who has played Joanne and been the show's
star since it premiered, certainly has to be considered
its spiritual leader.

Search for Tomorrow features rather mundane and
likeable Middle American families, but it has spiced
up their lives with murders, mafia dealings, attacks
of hysterical blindness, illegitimate children, and
financial wheelings and dealings among rich in-laws
that would turn any Getty or Rockefeller pale. The
story started with Joanne happily married to Keith

Barron, a young and handsome college graduate
from a wealthy family. Joanne was naive and shy by
comparison, of ordinary Midwestern stock. They
had a daughter, Patti.

When Keith died, his possessive mother instigated
everything from court procedures to kidnapping to
take Joanne's child away. But Joanne won out and, in
partnership with her close friends Stu and Marge
Bergman, opened Joanne Barron's Motor Haven
Inn. Joanne was being romanced by Arthur Tate at
the time, and Arthur got financing for the Motor

Lynn Loring, the actress who played Patti for twelve years, grew up on the show; she played the part from age five to eighteen. Memorizing Search *scripts was how she first learned to read.*

Stu and Marge Bergman (Larry Haines *and* Melba Rae) *became Joanne's closest friends and helped her once she became a widow.*

(L to r) Nathan Walsh (George Petrie), *Rose* (Nita Talbot), *and Joanne Barron. Joanne opened up the Motor Haven Inn in order to support herself once she had lost her husband. Rose later caused problems by poisoning a bowl of soup in order to ruin Joanne's reputation as an inn-keeper so that gangsters could take over the hotel and use it as a front.*

Joanne with daughter Patti and Arthur Tate (Karl Webber), who became Joanne's second husband. Eventually Arthur dropped dead of a heart attack.

Another Arthur Tate, this one played by Tony O'Sullivan.

Sam Reynolds (Bob Mandan) was husband number three for Joanne. He proved his love to her by saving her daughter from a knife-wielding drug addict. Later, just before they got married, Sam had to go off on business to Africa. He got lost in the jungle, was thought dead, and returned much later to Henderson mentally deranged from an African disease.

Haven from his rich Aunt Cornelia, an unscrupulous old lady who would later bring ruin on her own nephew. Meanwhile, naive Jo was taken by surprise when "the Syndicate" tried to take her new motel away from her to use as a front for illegal operations. Not only did they get Arthur's dead ex-wife's identical twin to try to take Arthur away, they arranged for an inside spy to get a job at the Motor Haven and poison a pot of soup.

Arthur and Joanne got married, but Arthur was sinking fast, overextending himself financially and becoming an alcoholic. When Joanne's jealous sister, Eunice, showed up in town, she succeeded in seducing him. More troubles followed, including the murder of Aunt Cornelia. Eventually, Arthur went to Alcoholics Anonymous and was on the way to recovery when a stranger arrived in town to sue him for paternity. Arthur had had enough. He fell dead of a heart attack, and Joanne was left twice widowed.

Enter Sam Reynolds, who had been Arthur's archenemy, to woo Joanne. But she wanted none of it until he was able to prove his devotion by risking his life to save her daughter, Patti, who had grown into a "beat generation" teenager, from a knife-wielding drug addict. Eunice, returned from a stay in Puerto Rico, attempted another sisterly seduction, but Sam was a stronger man than Arthur and turned her down. Then Sam went on trial for the murder of his ex-wife. Just as he was cleared and it looked like he and Joanne could marry, he was sent off to Africa to assist in a U.N. study, fell off a river boat, and was reported missing.

Joanne was blinded in a car accident and fell in love with her doctor, Tony Vincente. They were about to marry when Sam returned from Africa—alive but mentally deranged from the effects of jungle disease. Joanne, ever faithful, returned to Sam, only to end up being falsely accused of his murder. When she was cleared, she married Tony, but he died shortly after of a heart attack brought on

Husband number four was Tony Vincente (Tony George).

when he came to the rescue of a girl who was being menaced by members of ''the Mob.''

Joanne was now four times widowed. She turned to her old friend Stu Bergman, who by this time had lost his wife. The two, a good bit older and wiser now, renewed their strictly platonic friendship and went into business together again. This time they opened the Hartford House, a more modern version of the old Motor Haven Inn. New love affairs for Joanne followed, one with a writer named Chris Miller who bowed out to take care of his ailing wife,

another with Dr. Greg Hartford that was shaken repeatedly by the interference of his jealous and unstable daughter. Joanne Barron Tate Reynolds Vincente seems destined to be perpetually unlucky in love.

In the twenty-seven years that Mary Stuart has played the part of Joanne, she's gotten pregnant twice in real life. She didn't stop performing either time. The first time, she was supposed to be in the process of getting married to Arthur Tate in the story, so it was important that her condition be kept con-

Joanne and Tony Vincente went off on a honeymoon trip to the Carribean. They made a handsome couple, but not for long. He died of a heart attack after rescuing a girl from ''the Mob.''

After so many ill-fated love affairs and marriages, Joanne turned once again to finding a way to keep busy and support herself. With the help of Stu Bergman, now a widower, she opened up the Hartford House, a modern incarnation of the old Motor Haven Inn.

cealed. This was accomplished with the help of twelve-year-old daughter Patti, who was positioned standing in front of her mother all through her pregnancy so that all that ever showed on TV was Joanne's head and shoulders.

Mary's second real-life pregnancy was incorporated right into the storyline. Joanne got pregnant by husband Arthur, and as Mary Stuart got larger through the months, so did Joanne. When TV son Duncan Erik was born and shown in the hospital, it was actually Mary's own son who was seen; the TV crew filmed on-location shots of Mary with her baby. But the story turned sour when the writers of *Search* decided to have the new baby run out into the street

and get killed by a car. Mary was so infuriated by this storyline that she threatened to quit the show. Though she argued with the producers, she did not get her way, and later she told a reporter from *Afternoon TV* Magazine, "It was my own child. It had been a complicated pregnancy for me, and playing the death of the child was just too horrible to even consider. The show's ratings had been dropping, and I knew they were killing the child just to have something dramatic to boost the ratings. I played those scenes, all right, but I made them so horrifying that nobody could watch. Not even the make-up girl. She wouldn't even look at the monitor to see whether my make-up was right, it was too awful to watch. And

One of the new men in Joanne's life was Chris Miller (Paul Dumont), *a writer, who came to stay at Hartford House. Though hopes were high for another marriage, complications developed when Chris's estranged wife showed up in Henderson looking for him. It turned out she was sick with a fatal illness, and Chris had to leave Henderson to return to San Francisco and care for her.*

nobody out in televisionland watched either. It didn't help the ratings. In my own mind, I was remembering the morning my own father died. My mother just could never accept it. She'd walk around with a hopeful smile, in a daze, saying, 'He's going to get better. . . .' That's the way I played it. I destroyed them.''

More recently, *Search for Tomorrow,* like a number of other soaps, has expanded to a "layered" storyline designed to attract a wider spread of ages among viewers by involving characters of different ages in plotlines.

For the older set, steady and predictable stories center mostly around Joanne and her friends—Stu Bergman's new marriage to Ellie and John Wyatt's future following the murder of his wife, a "reclaimed" Eunice, by his jealous young lover.

Newer and more modern stories involve the younger generation of Henderson, such as Steve and Liza Kaslo, who have faced the problems of conflicting careers, infidelity, and personal tragedy.

The middle layer in the *Search* saga has revolved around such characters as Scott and Kathy Phillips. His recurrent alcoholism, her adultery and subsequent nervous breakdown, and their mutual long-standing difficulties with their adopted son, Eric, are just some of the problems that have befallen them in recent years.

This layered approach to the storyline seems to have been just what *Search* needed to boost itself out of a dip in ratings. Without giving up any of the classic soap fare of murder, insanity, and romantic jealousy, *Search* has been able to glide smoothly into more modern dilemmas that have succeeded in broadening its appeal.

"Happy Birthday, Search"

Search for Tomorrow celebrated its twenty-fifth anniversary on the air in September, 1976, making it the longest-running show in the television industry's history. The cast, their families and friends, CBS representatives, and representatives of Procter & Gamble Productions were all on hand for a black-tie birthday party at the Plaza Hotel. Mary Stuart, the star and longest running cast member of the show, gave the following speech to commemorate those years:

" Twenty-five years ago I turned a corner and came upon an empty space. . . . Three wise men, Charles Irving, Roy Winsor, and Bill Craig, coming from three separate directions, turned corners in their own lives at almost that same moment and came upon that same space. They had an idea. Where there had been nothing, we built a town. People came to live there; they married and had children. They built businesses; kids went to school and grew up. People moved there from other towns and it grew into a city . . . Oh, you can't find it on a map, and at night the houses and the shops come apart and are stored in scenery docks, but it is real. If you don't believe me, ask millions of people all over the country, and they will tell you it's real. Maybe a special kind of real that is a little gentler. It is a place to share a fantasy, an idea, a friend, or emotion. The emotions are not play-pretend; we all know that and so do they. If that is not reality, I don't know what is. Many beautiful people have passed through our town. Some, like ornamental trees, have blossomed for a season and gone on to bloom again or fade. A very special few have stayed and grown to giant shady trees. Yes, we have roots and a history. We have a present and a past . . . and we have a future, for we continue. We are happy never ending. We are a lovely place to go and where I want to be. Thank you for making that possible. . . ."

Search for Tomorrow's cast assembled at the 1976 celebration of the show's twenty-fifth birthday.

Joanne always gets along well with the young folks of Henderson. Here (l to r) are Gary Walton (Richard Lohman), Bruce Carson (Joel Higgins), Joanne (Mary Stuart), and Liza Kaslo (Meg Bennett).

Scott Phillips, played for many years by Peter Simon, and Kathy Phillips, played by Courtney Sherman, were married both on screen and off. In fact, they exchanged marriage vows a total of three times, twice in the storyline and once in real life.

Stephanie Collins (Marie Cheatham) *and David Sloan* (Lewis Arlt).

Liza Kaslo (played at the time by Meg Bennett) *and her husband, Steve* (Michael Nouri). *Steve had been trying to make it big as a songwriter. His lucky break came when Melissa Manchester (the real live singer) showed up in Henderson to hire him to play in her band.*

Joanne (Mary Stuart) *and Bruce Carson* (Joel Higgins).

MARY
Queen of Soaps

MARY STUART has played Joanne on *Search for Tomorrow* for over twenty-seven years. That makes her the longest-running television personality and perhaps the only person in all dramatic history to have played one character for over a quarter of a century.

We haven't met before, but Mary and I are about to spend the day together. When I step out of the cab in front of her Upper East Side apartment building, she is already coming through the door. She stops to consult with the doorman for a moment. The dog will

need walking, and she is nearly out of milk. As we turn to head down the sidewalk, she explains that the doorman is like a member of the family.

At the drugstore on Madison Avenue I stand watching as Mary cashes a check and chats with the druggist. It's clear he knows her, but I wonder if he also knows that this woman, with large and vulnerable eyes that make her look like Judy Garland, is one of the most popular actresses on daytime television.

Once outside we spot Pesya, the stately, gray-haired wardrobe mistress for *Search*. She and Mary share a cab to work each day, and the Checker she has already nabbed is waiting at the corner. Mary runs, and I am close behind her. We slam the door shut and speed downtown, three generations of working women in the unglamorous early stages of what will turn out to be a very long working day.

Mary Stuart grew up in Tulsa, Oklahoma, and lived through the poverty of the Depression and the dust storms of the dry plains. She once read a radio magazine that said that serial actresses earned $500 a week. As soon as she was old enough, she left Tulsa for New York City to launch a career as an actress. "No one in Tulsa spoke my language," she recalls. "And I thought all of New York was going to look like the inside of Radio City Music Hall." Her first job was as a hatcheck girl in the Roosevelt Grill. From time to time she'd sing with the band, and on one of those nights Hollywood producer Joe Pasternak, who happened to be in the audience, came up and told her, "You ought to be in movies."

By the next day he'd arranged a screen test, and shortly afterwards she was on her way to Hollywood, under contract to MGM, to begin four years as a starlet. Twenty films later, she suddenly quit her job, sold her house, and headed back to New York. She was prepared to start from scratch; Hollywood and the world of kidney-shaped swimming pools just hadn't suited her.

Back in New York, she found herself one afternoon in the awkward position of having to make small talk with a stranger named Roy Winsor while the two of them waited for a mutual friend for lunch.

Mary knew that Winsor had something to do with television, but she didn't know what. So to start conversation she said, "Women are too perfect on radio and television. Other women can't see themselves in these characters. Their needs aren't satisfied. Why can't television do something for them?" Some months later Winsor sent an assistant to track her down. He had created a new serial and designed the lead for the lady he had met at lunch. This was 1951. Winsor may not have read the same magazine Mary had as a young girl in Tulsa, but he *had* instructed his assistant to offer her a salary of $500 a week to start.

The rehearsal hall where Mary waits with her fellow cast members to run through the day's lines is a windowless cinder-block room cluttered with the regulation coffee urn, boxes of donuts, metal folding chairs, and Formica tables. Two actors stand in the middle of the floor rehearsing when director Don Wallace breaks the action. "Hey, Mary," he calls, "have we ever played the kitchen down here?" He points to a place on the floor. Mary, who knows more about the history of Henderson than any other person involved in the making of the show, shakes her head and points farther up the floor.

When it comes time for her scene, she takes her place. Joanne's storyline for the day will have her face the fact that she's about to lose yet another lover. Chris Miller, who has wooed her while staying as a guest at her hotel, is about to return to his estranged wife. The reason for this sudden shift in storyline is that after Paul Dumont, the actor who plays Chris, had been brought on to be Joanne's new "love interest," it was discovered that the two didn't get along very well.

Paul Dumont and Mary Stuart now sit opposite each other in metal chairs. Mary reads her first line. "I can't help wondering what happened when you told her you'd take her back to San Francisco."

"She was relieved and delighted. At first," reads Dumont.

"Oh?" Mary looks up at her fellow actor. Her eyes widen.

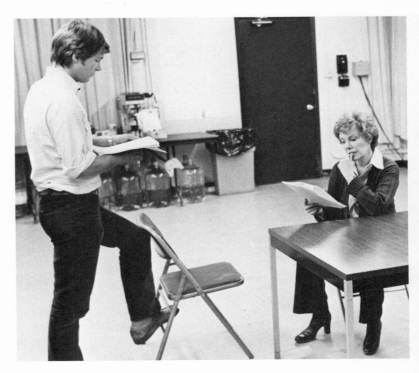

"Till she found out that I planned to come back here as soon as she saw her own doctor."

"You went into that too?"

"She thought I meant I was going back to our old life together. I had to tell her I was returning to Henderson in three or four days."

"That must have been a double blow," reads Mary, slowing down a bit now as she comes across a line that troubles her. "Just when you'd given her some hope . . . she's so alone now. And she may be facing a death sentence she knows nothing about."

Mary stops and grimaces. She looks at director Don Wallace. "Isn't that line just a bit too much?" While Wallace reviews the lines in the script, Mary offers, "How about, 'She's so alone right now. And she's desperately ill. . . .'" Wallace agrees to the change. He calls to his assistant, who sits with the script and a stopwatch at a side table, "Did you get that?" Dumont clears his throat and begins again. Though he's trying hard to mask it, he has that humbled look of a soap opera actor who knows his days on a show are quickly coming to an end.

Upstairs in her dressing room Mary sits in front of the mirror, looks at herself, her hair, her skin, then

stops and stares a moment at the telephone. She takes her copy of the day's script and flattens it out in front of her. There's a checklist on the cover page where she's penciled her chores for the day. "I have to call *TV Guide*. I did a phone interview with them yesterday and I made a few mistakes. I hate phone interviews."

The dressing room is so small that we sit nearly knee to knee. The metal closet doors are standing open and the clothes inside overflow. Along the wall there's a row of hooks with umbrellas, sweaters, hats, and dresses that look like they've been there for months. Lately Mary's been busy with her second career as a singer and songwriter, and now she explains to the reporter on the other end of the phone, " . . . and did I tell you the show is funny? My musical arranger told me to be sure to tell you it's funny. It seems like a strange thing to say, but I *am* funny. I mean the show is funny, it's funny. . . ."

When she hangs up the phone, she looks back into the mirror. At that moment she doesn't look funny at all; she looks strangely alone and sad. "You know, it's about three in the morning that I start thinking about everything I didn't do right in the day." Mary turns away from the mirror. She unpacks her guitar and places it in her lap, as if it were a friend that could comfort her. She strums a moment and hums a melody. "Three in the morning is when you go over

every last detail in your head. You know, I wrote a book once, a children's book, and there was a publisher who wanted to buy it from me if I would make some revisions. When I told my husband about it he threw the book across the room and yelled, 'How do you expect to write a book if you've never read one?' I never finished it, but you know, the day I divorced my husband was the day I wrote and sang my first song."

In the make-up room Mary climbs up into the barber chair. Joel Mason is ready to make her up to look like Joanne, as he has done morning after morning for years.

In the early years of *Search for Tomorrow*, Mary Stuart's responsibility extended beyond acting. She also saw to the accuracy of her scenes by shopping herself for the props she would need, and she insisted that food served in her "kitchen" was homemade. Mary has always been intensely committed to her portrayal of the role of Joanne, and the character has changed and developed in response to changes in the actress's own life. When Mary divorced, she celebrated her new independence by cutting her long hair into a new and more stylish hairdo. The character of Joanne had been known for her homely bun and the sewing basket she carried everywhere so her free moments could be used in mending old clothes. Once the actress cut her hair the show's writers had to incorporate the more modern style into the story. They wrote a scene in which Joanne shyly untied a kerchief to show off her new hairdo. For both the actress and the character, this signaled a big change in personality. Mary had decided to strike out on her own, and the character of Joanne concurrently became more outspoken, adventuresome, and independent.

Mary and I sit side by side on a bed on the studio set and eat roast beef sandwiches for lunch. The empty set is quiet; the technicians are out on lunch break, and for a few moments we have Henderson to ourselves.

"It's really not like being two people," Mary says. "It's not as simple as that. You see, it's as if we've grown up together. I've put myself into

Joanne, and she in turn has helped me grow. Through her I've been able to try out new aspects of myself. As I tried to become more independent in my own life, I put the same things into her, and as they worked in her, they strengthened my ability to carry on with the independence I was also choosing for myself. When I try something out in Joanne and I get good feedback on it, it gives me the courage to try it out in myself in real life.'' Mary pauses to consider something, then says, ''You know, I meet people at parties, and when they hear I'm a soap opera actress, they can hardly conceal their condescension. They say things like, 'Oh, yes, well, my maid watches those shows.' In this country we're all programed not to show feelings, and soap operas are all about feelings. That's why people put them down. That's why they're ashamed to say they watch them.''

Bright lights suddenly come on and the technicians and cameramen pour into the studio. Cued by the arrival of the crew, Mary stands, wraps the rest of her sandwich in waxed paper, and goes to sit in the chair from which she'll be playing her day's scenes. She sits alone quietly, as if making some internal transition to the sad, subdued Joanne who is preparing to say goodbye to yet another man.

In the control booth, scenes come through on the monitors. Mary loses her lover, cries with her friend Ellie, sings a song of loneliness. When the thirty minutes are up, Mary arrives at the door of the control room. Don Wallace turns to her and smiles. Another successful day in Henderson.

After a quick sitting for pictures with photographers from *Soap Opera Digest,* Mary has me by the hand and we're back on the street hailing a cab for the ride uptown. She's already late for the afternoon rehearsal with her musicians. Henderson fades as we speed up Sixth Avenue and Mary leans back, folds her hands in her lap, and shuts her eyes for the ride.

Back at Mary's apartment, her mother insists I see the collection of fan mail that's been her responsibility to sort and file through the years. She has the letters organized in large boxes by date and subject matter. Nearly all are addressed to Joanne. There are the letters asking Joanne's advice, others offering her

support, and still others writing as if she were a friend. Some letters have come airmail special delivery and warn of dangers the viewers see mounting in Henderson.

From the next room the sound of Mary's singing voice draws me to stand at the doorway to watch her. She sits at the far end of the room, cradling her guitar, the late afternoon light casting shadows against her face. She sings words to songs she has written herself—songs telling of a struggle for independence, self-confidence, and lasting relationships.

As I stand there I notice something odd. Mary hasn't changed her clothes all day, not even to go on stage and play the part of Joanne. Mary Stuart and Joanne Vincente are not exactly the same person, yet it seems they both share a similar mix of personal determination and vulnerability. The irony is striking: Mary Stuart, who seems alone and lonely even when surrounded by people, is probably the only person in the world who has ever had eight million people who consider her their personal friend.

LARRY HAINES/STU BERGMAN: SOAP OPERA ACTING

Larry Haines (Stu Bergman).

Larry Haines plays Stu Bergman, a very likeable man who's been Joanne Vincente's closet friend for years. In addition to doing Search, *Haines is well known for his voiceovers on television commercials, guest appearances on nighttime shows, Broadway plays, and Hollywood films. In the following interview he talks about what it means to be a soap opera actor.*

QUESTION: How did you start acting?

LARRY HAINES: *I saw my first movie when I was seven—it might have been* The Big Parade, *something like that—and I fell madly in love with movies. I used to go to a Saturday matinee and sit through the picture twice. Then I'd go home and re-enact it all for the other kids in the neighborhood. That's how I got hooked on acting. In college I got a dramatic scholarship, and that made me think that maybe I was good enough to go ahead and try it professionally, so I made the rounds of the advertising agencies in New York. In those days they used to have what they called general auditions. You'd*

write for an appointment and bring in your own material. They had a rating system—good, bad, indifferent—and if you passed their audition, they'd cast you in whatever productions they had. Before I knew it I was doing three or four shows a day, seven days a week.

QUESTION: How did you end up on a soap?

HAINES: *I was on the very first soap opera on network television, a show called* The First Hundred Years. *When the producer on* Search *heard that* Hundred Years *was going off the air, he asked if I'd like to do a few shots on his show. The few shots developed into more than a twenty-five-year run.*

QUESTION: Does soap acting differ from the other kinds of acting you've done?

HAINES: *The really big difference is the speed with which you have to prepare. We start at eight in the morning and we block each scene and each act in the rehearsal hall, without camera, until about a quarter to ten. Then we go to make-up, and we're due on the set for camera rehearsal at ten-fifteen. We do a rough run-through of each scene, going through the whole show, and then do it again at eleven-thirty. We break at twelve for lunch, come back at one for "notes," dress rehearse at one-thirty, and tape from two-thirty to three. We do a half-hour show with roughly four hours of preparation.*

The last time I did Maude *I counted up the hours and it came to about forty-four or fourty-five hours of preparation—five or six days of work—of constant rewrites, constant rehearsing and polishing. By the time you get to taping, you're infinitely more prepared and secure in what you're doing than you are when you do a soap. On a soap you just have to be a very fast study. You have to take changes sometimes within minutes of final taping. If we come out of dress rehearsal one minute too long, they cut lines, and you have to take the cut, in your own mind erase what you've rehearsed before, and be ready with the change. I've seen famous people, well-established stars from other media, crack under the strain. The crucial thing in soaps is concentration, because if you're not with it you can blow lines.*

QUESTION: I've noticed that there's always a lot of wisecracking and goofing off around the set.

HAINES: *There's a lot of tension in the work, and the only way you can get rid of it is to kid around and feel as loose as you possibly can. Otherwise you just wouldn't be able to stand the strain. Luckily, we have a cast which is adaptable and rather loose, and we all get along well.*

QUESTION: I've heard that on some soaps new actors are ostracized at first—that they have to earn their way in.

HAINES: *I think the only time that happens is when a*

particular individual ostracizes himself but it's a natural thing when you come into a stock company that has played together for years to feel a little uptight at first.

QUESTION: One thing I'm curious about—writers come and go on the show and so do directors. You probably know more about your character than the writer ever could know.

HAINES: That's a problem on soaps. As an actor you have to learn to override the fluctuations in how your character is written. You have to inject your own knowledge of the character.

QUESTION: How do you do that?

HAINES: You do it in your playing attitude or sometimes by paraphrasing a line or two. Stu is not a college professor, but there have been writers in the past who've tried to write him that way. He's a self-made man, a kinetic kind of guy with a good sense of humor who likes to kid around. He's not up on etiquette or the proper thing to do all the time. He's just a human being. That's why I like playing him. He can also be extremely sensitive to people's problems, and he's capable of very deep feeling for those who mean anything to him. He's sincere, but he's square.

QUESTION: Don't you get tired of playing the same character every day?

HAINES: No. Sometimes I get a little annoyed when there isn't something interesting for me in terms of storyline and all I have to do is recap. Yet recapping is a necessary evil on soaps. You can't expect even an addicted fan to see five shows a week, so you have to catch him up on what he's missed. Joanne and I get a lot of the recapping scenes, and the trick is to make them sound conversational.

I don't like to read ahead, either. If we get the scripts in advance, I won't look at the next day's show until I've put the one we're doing totally "in the can." I play it as if each day—each episode—is a new day. There's a danger in reading ahead. They told me way in advance that I was going to end up marrying Ellie, but I would have preferred it if they hadn't. In the scenes I played leading up to it I already knew the ending. It made it much more difficult to act as if I didn't. In soaps it's best not to know.

QUESTION: Do people in real life sometimes expect you to react like Stu?

HAINES: All the time. I'd say that 90 percent of the ardent viewers of Search for Tomorrow don't want to think of Stu Bergman as a character played by an actor; they want to think of him as a real person who's actually going through all these things. When they stop me for an autograph, it's always, "Hey, Stu, how are you?" I try to be Stu while I'm talking with them, to be the same kind of guy. I try to keep it real for them. To my way of thinking, that's what makes or breaks a soap. The viewer has to accept the character as real. They want to be able to say, "Gee, I have a cousin like that," or "Isn't that just like my father?"

QUESTION: How has doing Search affected your career?

HAINES: It's been very important in this respect: had I not had the financial security of Search for Tomorrow, I would have had to take whatever other jobs were thrown my way and do them in order to eke out a living. The fact that I have had the security of Search means that I could afford to pick and choose what other shows I wanted or did not want to do. The result is that every show I've done on Broadway, with only one exception, has been a smash hit.

It's also been good for me because of the notoriety involved and the recognition. Once I was walking up the street when Joe DiMaggio passed me, and we hadn't gone more than maybe five steps beyond each other when we both simultaneously turned to look back. I got such a big kick out of the fact that Joe DiMaggio watched Search. My heart was pounding because he's my big hero and I had been too shy to stop him and ask for an autograph. Another time I was walking down Park Avenue when a limousine pulled up in front of a residential hotel. The then-Vice President of the United States and his wife, Mr. and Mrs. Nixon, got out of the car, and as I walked by I overheard Pat whispering in her husband's ear, "Hey, that's Stu Bergman—that's Stu on Search for Tomorrow."

The Soap Opera Kid

Chris Lowe is fourteen years old. For the last nine years of his life, he's had a double personality. He's a young boy who likes Elton John, eel fishing, and bike riding, and who goes to school with friends on Long Island; he's also Eric Phillips, who lives a traumatized life of alcoholic parents, divorce, remarriage, and illegitimacy in a town called Henderson. There are two similarities between the two boys: They both spend an unusual amount of time with adults rather than children their own age, and they both have personalities with a pensive side and an uncanny maturity for their young years.

Soap operas are about families and families have children, so the child actor is part of any soap cast, and some have played their roles for the greater portion of their own real lives. Inevitably they become mascots, not only of their own casts but of the whole subculture of soap opera. They are endeared by soap opera fan magazine reporters when they come up with answers like young Cathy Greene (Sally Spencer on Another World) did when asked how old she was. "Oh," Cathy said, throwing her long blonde hair back in an intimate gesture she must have learned from her longtime screen guardian, Jacqueline Courtney, "I don't believe I wish to establish that."

Children in soap operas present a tricky problem for the writers of the stories. Since it's difficult to create storylines for children who are too young, the writers tend to make the characters age faster than they would in real time. Many child actors can't keep up with the aging process of the characters they play and eventually have to be replaced by older actors.

More than once a youngster has dropped out of the story with no particular explanation, only to appear two years later as a young man ready to embark on a medical career. Others, notably Lynne Loring, who played Joanne's daughter, Patti, on Search for Tomorrow from the time she was six to sixteen, kept pace with their characters.

The way Chris Lowe first got into "the business" is a story so ordinary it's nearly unbelievable. As a toddler he was the sort everyone took an immediate liking to—blond with a ready smile and a vocabulary beyond his years. At age five, when he saw a TV commercial that warned of the dangers of cigarettes, he went on a campaign to stop adults from smoking. One place he carried his campaign to was the family swimming club, and one woman he approached with the warning, "It's a matter of life and breath," took such a liking to the boy that she insisted Chris's mother send his picture to a New York agent she knew of who handled child actors.

Anne Lowe sent off two snapshots of her son; months later she received a phone call asking her to bring Chris in to be seen. She dressed him up in a suit and tie and off the two went on the train to Manhattan. Chris's first professional audition was at the studio of Search for Tomorrow. Young boys and their mothers filled the casting office, everyone appearing to be veterans except Chris and Anne Lowe, who stood nervously hand-in-hand at one corner of the room. Suddenly Chris spotted a man smoking a cigarette, marched over to him, and warned, "It's a matter of life and breath!" The man turned out to be Search's producer, and Chris, for his impertinence, won the part of Eric.

Even at age five there was acting craft to be learned. Anne helped him memorize lines, the two working together for days before each show. Gradually his fellow actors taught him the trade. Lelia Scala, who played his grandmother, taught him to "run lines." Dan Levin, Chris's first director, who always addressed him formally, exactly the way he did the older actors, told him, "Mr. Lowe, you must always play with love!" Until he left the show, Peter Simon, Chris's on-screen adopted father, was his mentor.

Every child actor comes with a "stage mother." Some are so anxious to keep their children at work that they either try to keep them looking young so they'll be eligible for younger parts or make them look old so they'll seem more mature. Anne Lowe is an exception to this. She was a teacher before she retired to become Chris's stage mother, and she's used all her best knowledge of childhood development to keep the unusual circumstances of her son's life from hurting him. In addition to keeping track of his rehearsal schedules, helping him learn lines, transporting him to the studio and back, and shopping for his wardrobe, Anne tutors him on missed schoolwork. By special arrangement, Chris has no contract with Search. "I did this," his mother explains, "to be sure that if it ever got to be too much for him or I saw it hurting him in any way, I would be able to pull him right out."

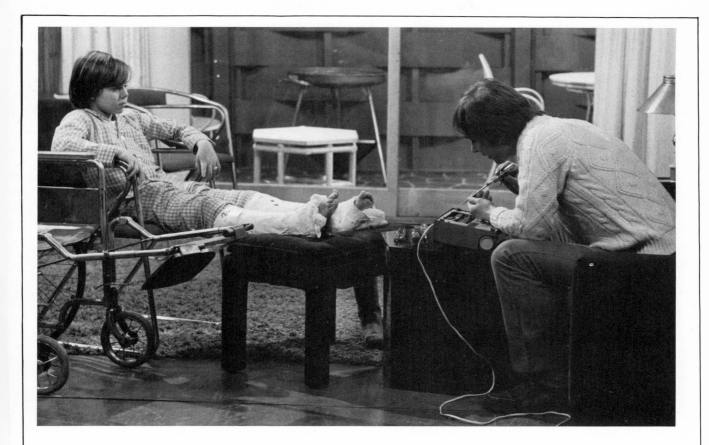

Like many other child actors, Chris also does television commercials. According to Chris, commercials are "the business," Search is "the show," and he clearly prefers the latter. "Once I did a Duncan Hines commercial where I must have had to eat a hundred brownies with a big grin on my face and say, 'Fudgey good!'" But commercials are where the big money is. A successful spot can earn him as much as $6000.

Chris is a disarming blend of child and adult. Sometimes he grins shyly like the fourteen-year-old boy he is; at other times he poses so serenely it's clear he's been in front of cameras for years.

His future? Chris folds his hands in his lap and takes a moment to think it through. "Well, I just want to live a normal life, I guess. I'd like to be an actor, or a director, or maybe a teacher like my father. But if I do go on with acting, I don't want to be a big star like John Wayne and live in Hollywood. I just want to be a normal person and live in my own house."

The test of Chris's acting ability came when he had to play scenes with his "drunken" father in a storyline about alcoholism. In the culmination of the episode, Chris as Eric portrayed Eric's sadness at seeing his father drunk and suddenly burst into tears. When he walked off the set after taping, the whole cast of Search gathered round. Chris was no longer just a cute child star who had gotten a part as a five-year-old; he had proved his mettle as an actor.

Eric Phillips (Chris Lowe) *and his adopted father, Scott Phillips* (Peter Simon). *"A young actor like Chris becomes aware of the process of acting as he begins to grow older. Chris is now starting to understand that he can control things within himself and he's being asked to do it a lot more. He's being asked to show emotions that four years ago he didn't even know existed. For example, he's learning to summon up great sadness, and he's doing it the right way without anybody teaching him how. He's learning that he has a lot of real emotions within himself that he can control and use in acting. He wasn't aware of this before. It's a very confusing time for an actor, and he's getting through it well."* —PETER SIMON

As The World Turns

AS THE WORLD TURNS is the old-fashioned soap opera. It premiered on CBS in 1956, and according to Helen Wagner, who has played Nancy Hughes of Oakdale since the show's beginning, it "has accomplished what people have been trying to accomplish on stage since the time of the Greeks—pure identification between the audience and the character." The "stage" is the kitchen table; instead of hemlock or strange elixirs, the characters rely on coffee; but the lives of people in Oakdale reflect the old-fashioned virtues. Marriages, children, and family are what keep it turning; the incest, drug addiction, war protest, and abortions of some of the other shows have no place here. *As The World Turns* is

The family: Nancy, Chris, and Don Hughes. Richard Holland played the part of Don from the time of his validictorian speech in high school until the earning of his law degree.

nostalgia of an earlier, and perhaps more sensible, era in American history.

This soap hangs on to such vestiges of the past as the family doctor who makes house calls and wants to hear not only about your symptoms but your home life. Dr. Dan Stewart is known to stop in unannounced just to check up on how his patients are doing, and Dr. Bob Hughes is never rushed and rarely has to consult a file to recall information about a patient's case.

As The World Turns also hangs on to virtue. For example, even though bratty Lisa caused the Hughes family endless troubles, she was still a welcome family friend. Nancy Hughes, Lisa's ex-mother-in-law, doesn't hold old grudges and thus shows the younger folks the value of forgiveness. Every day, viewers get a dose of old American values. Right below the surface of the stories are the messages of

Don Hughes (played at this time by Richard Holland) *is shown with his grandfather, Grandpa Hughes* (Santos Ortega), *and his parents, Chris and Nancy Hughes* (Don MacLaughlin *and* Helen Wagner). *Don and Helen still play their parts after twenty-two years on the show, and they're still, by some soapland miracle, happily and successfully married.*

A convocation of Oakdale lawyers: (l to r) Judge Lowell (William Johnstone), *Chris Hughes, and Mitchell Drew* (Geoffrey Lumb).

any minister's Sunday sermons. Women who try to break up marriages are scorned and eventually ostracized; men of character are good fathers to their children; and women who work never do so at the expense of their husbands or their children.

As writers of *As The World Turns,* husband and wife team Edith Sommer and Robert Soderberg acknowledge this aspect of their stories. "We do feel morality is involved. The audience wants our characters to do the decent thing whenever possible, and if we don't live up to that, they let us know."

As The World Turns was an Irna Phillips creation, and as such it represents the family theme she injected into all her shows. Its large and loyal audience, many of whom are in the over-fifty age bracket, probably began watching the show when their husbands brought home the first family TV set. Then they had school-age children and were busy with homemaking chores. Now, like their friend Nancy of Oakdale, they look forward to holidays when grandchildren come to visit. *As The World Turns* plays particularly to this older audience. It doesn't shock

and it doesn't try to educate. It doesn't try to come up with melodramatic storylines. Instead, it's a reassuring visit with old friends whom viewers have come to know over years of watching. As always, they carry on the events of their daily lives. The Fourth of July picnic in Oakdale is as important an event as mental breakdowns and divorces are in some of the other soap towns.

As The World Turns features families with white Anglo-Saxon names like Stewart, Hughes, Lowell, and Colman. There are no blacks to speak of and no ethnic diversity. According to one actor on the show, "Every time we try a minority group story, it doesn't work. We just don't get the ratings." Nobody in Oakdale is particularly poor. Of the two original main families, the Lowells and the Hugheses, the Lowells were rich and unhappy, the Hugheses were middle class and stable. This is typical of the traditionally soapy themes that teach not only that riches do not necessarily bring happiness, but that despite class differences, everyone can get along and be friends.

(L to r) Chris Hughes, Lisa Hughes (Eileen Fulton), *and Nancy Hughes. Lisa eloped with Chris and Nancy's son Bob while he was supposed to be pursuing his studies at college. At first the Hugheses were incensed, but when Lisa announced that she was pregnant, Nancy invited Lisa and Bob to move in with them into the family house. According to Helen Wagner: "The trouble with Lisa was that she was always interested in life, and the more that was going on the better as far as she was concerned. If things slowed down to a walk, she got restless, and then she'd go out and stir up some excitement."*

Grandpa Hughes (here with Lisa) was the understanding philosopher of the Hughes household. When Santos Ortega, the actor who played the part, took ill and it seemed likely that he would die, the show's writers decided to have Grandpa marry and go off to live with his new wife on a farm with his son John. This way when Ortega did die, the actors who had come to be his close friends and colleagues over the years were spared having to deal with Grandpa's death in the storyline until some months after the death of the actor himself.

When Ellen (Wendy Drew, right) found out she was pregnant, she didn't tell anyone about it except for her friend Penny (Rosemary Prinz, left). Even though she wasn't married, Ellen wanted to keep her baby, and when the pregnancy started to show, she left Oakdale and had the baby where no one would know. In the end she did give it up for adoption, and though she didn't know it until later, the baby's adopted parents became an Oakdale couple, Betty and David Stewart. They named the new baby Dan.

AS THE WORLD TURNS 63

Over time, the Lowell family died out, leaving only a daughter named Ellen in Oakdale. Meanwhile, the Hughes family grew strong, with Chris and Nancy Hughes heading an ever-enlarging clan with three children—Penny, Bob, and Don—who all have gone on to raise families of their own. Chris Hughes still runs the law practice that he started long ago with Jim Lowell. Nancy's sole career in life has been to nurture and support her family.

The first big upset for Nancy Hughes came when her son Bob, a college student with great profes-

sional promise, ran off and eloped with a tempestuous young girl from a poorer background. After much heartbreak, all was forgiven and Bob and Lisa returned to live in Oakdale in the family home. But Lisa was bored with the life of a housewife and daughter-in-law and went looking for new men to liven up her life. Their marriage soon ended in divorce. Both Lisa and Bob got married again, but their second marriages failed as well. Lisa and Bob's son, Tom, grew up to have even worse marital luck. The Hughes's other son, Don, also seemed destined

Penny and Jeff (Mark Rydell) *ran off and eloped without telling anybody about their plans, but after awhile their marriage was annulled and they split apart. Later the couple got back together, and this time they had a magnificent formal wedding. They were married by Sydney Lanier, a minister in real life who appeared on* As the World Turns *from time to time to marry couples, even though usually he was busy with his own parish, the St. Thomas Church on Fifth Avenue in New York City.*

After much more than their share of problems, Lisa and Bob broke up, and Lisa went off to live on her own. According to one of her admirers, "Lisa Hughes was always my favorite character on soap opera. She was so bad you just had to love her. I mean she could make you hate her so much, she was that good. She just made you believe she was the rottenest thing."

for endless romantic mishaps, the latest in his marriage to Joyce, who wasted no time before causing him grief both financially and emotionally.

Stable home life and the price paid when that stability is upset is an underlying concern of everyone in Oakdale. Nancy and Chris's marriage is the example of what is possible if two people love each other with the proper respect and forgiveness. The young folks, by contrast, are all too impatient, unwilling to put in the hard work it takes to make marriages succeed, and are destined to wreck havoc on themselves and their children.

Another theme of life in Oakdale is that though ambition is good, and striving to improve economically is the American way, overambitiousness can

destroy everything worth having—love, success, and family happiness. Misguided John Dixon, for example, constructed a lie to try to oust his competitor, Dr. Bob Hughes, from his post at the hospital. John wanted to move up in the world, but instead of getting there by hard work he tried to do it through conniving. People who exercise bad judgment in soaps always have to pay the price, and so when John was caught he lost not only his wife but his medical practice. Through losing everything, he earned a chance to start all over again and learn from his mistakes. Soap opera always allows people who pay the price for their misdeeds to earn a second chance.

When Nancy and Chris Hughes celebrated their twentieth wedding anniversary on the air, the show asked viewers to send in cards of congratulations, and the mail arrived in bushels. Nancy and Chris have one of the few marriages in the world of soaps that seems to endure. Once when one of the show's writers insinuated that Chris Hughes had eyes for another woman, viewers expressed such outrage that another such plot has never been considered.

Characters that have been around as long as these become symbols. Irna Phillips understood this soapy phenomenon by which characters she created often grew larger than life, and she dealt with them in a manner equally as grandiose.

When Jim Lowell was "killed off" on *As The World Turns,* and there was a terrible uproar among viewers who wrote in to the program and to her to protest the demise of one of their favorite characters, Irna responded in nearly God-like tones. She sent a written message back to the protesting viewers: ". . . As the world turns, we know the bleakness of

> *"My momma used to tell us to go play cause she was napping. Then she'd go to her room, lie down on her bed, and turn on the TV to watch* As the World Turns. *When I started watching too, my momma and I had something to talk about."*
>
> *"My father-in-law watched* As the World Turns *for years. Then one of the characters was sent to jail for something she didn't do and he was so angry and upset about it that he turned off the TV and has refused to watch ever since."*

winter, the promise of spring, the fullness of summer, and the harvest of autumn . . . the cycle of life is completed. . . . What is true of nature is also true of man. He too has a cycle."

As The World Turns has given birth to a number of very popular daytime stars. Among them is Rosemary Prinz, who played the role of Penny Hughes for many years. The actress's feelings about soap opera were always ambivalent, and when she finally quit

Eventually Lisa settled down with Grant Colman (James Douglass), *but for a long time his ex-wife, Joyce* (Barbara Rodell), *was always coming between them. Joyce finally gave up and married Don Hughes.*

*Kim (Kathryn Hays) and John Dixon (Larry Bryggman). "John Dixon loved Kim dearly, and he married her knowing she didn't love him. Then instead of doing what he knew would please her, he went out and pursued his own ambitions. That was the kind of man he was, even to the point of attacking Bob Hughes in order to try to get the position of Chief of Staff at the hospital, and Kim knew better than to believe the lies John was telling about Bob. If John had taken the time to sit down and think out what he was doing, he would have seen how wrong he was. But on soap opera you follow through on what happens to a character. In the case of John Dixon, he doesn't just get his comeuppance, the curtain goes down, and everyone goes home for the evening. No, you go on. You have to deal with what happens to him when he gets his just desserts. How's he going to handle it? Is he going to change? That's the great strength of this medium. You follow through and find out what happens to a person. That's what 'tune in tomorrow' is all about." —*HELEN WAGNER *(Nancy Hughes)*

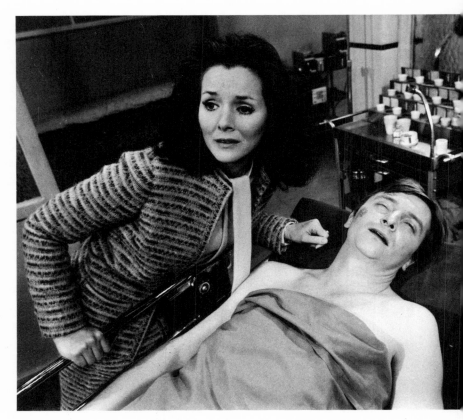

the show for good, she publicly swore off a daytime career. At a press conference she told reporters, "I feel like I have come out of a crowded room and can take a breath of fresh air." Much later, she did return to a soap, but only for a brief time and as a personal favor.

Eileen Fulton, as troublesome, troublemaking Lisa, became another enormously popular soap opera star. She has played the part from the very early stages of her acting career, and her own willfulness and imagination were instrumental in making Lisa into the tempestuous character she became. Actually, the part of Lisa was originally meant to be one of

"When my marriage broke up I was depressed and I didn't have a job, so I'd stay home and watch soap operas. I'd never watched them before, but at that time it was just about all I could manage. They gave me something to hang onto when everything else in my life was falling apart."

a sweet and agreeable girl. It was Eileen herself, sick of her own upbringing as the well-behaved daughter of a small-town minister, who decided to give the part a touch of the renegade. The result was that Lisa turned into one of soapland's most popular bitches.

More recently, Kathryn Hays, playing the role of Kim, has also become a very popular daytime star. Kim was one of the last characters created by Irna Phillips, brought to life in the final stages of her writing career and shortly before her own death. Irna said of the character, "Kim Reynolds . . . is really me—at a much younger age. She's fiercely independent, as I was, and she won't settle for second best. She's having a child out of wedlock that will be only hers; I adopted two children—Cathy and Tommy—without having a husband. We're both the same. And she's going to have that child to prove that a woman can do it alone." The character of Kim demonstrated a graceful self-possession that quickly won the hearts of viewers.

In recent years, Oakdale has seen its share of love triangles. Kim, who married John Dixon to give her child a father, fell in love with Dan Stewart, but Dan's ex-wife Susan was determined to keep them apart. Among other nasty tricks, she pulled off a Watergate-like caper, stealing a tape cassette from Dan's answering machine so he would leave Oakdale without ever knowing Kim had regained her lost memory and knew she loved him. The trick didn't work for long, however, and Kim and Dan were eventually married.

Meanwhile, Grant Colman wanted to marry Lisa, but Joyce, his former wife, wouldn't have it. She tried everything from an attack of appendicitis to claims of a child by Grant to get him back. Lisa, mellowed now after so many years of causing trouble, was the good one in this triangle, and as soap opera fate often has it, by being good she won the man. Much later, a new triangle was created when her son Chuck was killed and her older son Tom severely injured in a car accident. Lisa found herself being drawn to Tom's father, Bob Hughes, as a result of the tragedy. Her marriage broke up over it, but she eventually reconciled with Grant.

The younger generation of Oakdale residents has also gotten into the act. For example, Anne and Dee Stewart, the two daughters of David and Ellen's former marriage, went off to college together and fell in love with the same man, a graduate law student named Beau Spencer. Anne finally won that battle and married him.

"Bloopers"

Time and money are the biggest problems faced in producing soaps, and this often means that mistakes made by actors cannot be retaped and corrected. In the days of live production there was never a chance to correct mistakes. Actors had to be prepared to ad lib a missed line or quickly figure out how to pantomine using a prop that was not on the set. Soap opera history is full of "bloopers."

Once when the Hughes family in As the World Turns was having one of its annual picnics in the backyard, poor Tom Hughes walked away with the grass, a synthetic product that hadn't been properly glued onto the floor.

Door handles have come off in actors' hands. Lights have been kept from falling by adroit actors who propped up the lightstand with a foot while nonchalantly delivering lines. Telephones haven't been where they were supposed to be so that actors had to pantomime dialing.

Val Dufour, in his early soap days, played jet engineer Zack James on a show called First Days. Fridays are always days for cliff-hangers on soaps, and on this Friday Val was to witness a terrible plane crash, hurry back home to his wife, and frantically tell her, "Chris cracked up the plane!" Only when he rushed onto the scene he found himself announcing, "Chris crapped . . . up the plane." It was a live show. There was no turning back.

But even though all this romantic intrigue keeps life moving along in Oakdale, in fact it's only a backdrop for the real stuff and character of the show. *As The World Turns* is primarily a calm and endearing portrayal of ordinary middle-class life, or what middle-class life once was in America. As the archtypical Irna Phillips creation, drama and action are almost superfluous; it's people—their foibles, interests, habits, and worries—that make the world turn.

DRESSING
ROOM
DRAMA

Production Date: Thursday, July 20
Air Date: October
Script Number: 007
Network: CBS
Cast:
   Helen Wagner
   Don MacLaughlin
   Interviewer

FADE IN:

A dressing room made of gray cinder blocks tucked amidst the maze of studios, dressing rooms, rehearsal halls, and offices that make up the CBS Broadcast Center on West 57th Street in New York City. This dressing room belongs to Helen Wagner, who has just arrived to change out of the clothes she wore to portray Nancy Hughes of Oakdale. A stack of opened letters—the week's fan mail—is piled neatly in front of the mirror. There's the script, marked up and tattered, from the day's work. A cot is covered with a woven spread, and behind it on the wall, a framed embroidery reminds: "Home Is Where the Heart Is."

Helen greets the interviewer. Like her on-screen counterpart, Helen is kind and attentive.

There's a knock on the door and Don MacLaughlin arrives. He's the actor who plays Chris Hughes, Helen's on-screen husband of more than twenty years. Together, they hold the record for longevity in soap opera marriages.

Helen greets Don with a warm and approving smile. They've have been working together as a team for the greater part of both of their professional lives.

Don is a bit sheepish because he had forgotten about the time of the interview and had to be reminded by a phone call from Helen. It's not so different from how things might have worked out in Oakdale, where Nancy Hughes keeps things running smoothly while Chris, a little less organized, is the one who always offers sage advice.

Interviewer: *Chris and Nancy's marriage on* As The World Turns *seems to be the only one on television that works.*

Don: *I suppose we're fairly unique that way. It's a good point for a soap opera to make—that two people can be happily married. If everyone in the whole town is getting divorced and remarried all the time, it tends to become unreal. I'm not saying that our storyline is just reeking with reality, but I do think it's pretty true to life. Our show isn't really like a play, it's more like a visit with next-door neighbors.*

I spoke the other day with someone who is working both on our show and on Edge of Night, *and he said he's been trying to get an understanding of the difference between the two shows. If I can paraphrase what he said, it was that he felt* Edge of Night *is built on hate because they're always out to get each other. You know, there's a tremen-*

dous amount of animosity and violence on that show. He felt that As The World Turns was different because instead of animosity, it is based on love.

HELEN: *He said that originally he had thought it was all romantic love, but over time he realized it was much more. It is caring for people, caring for friends, the kind of caring that shows in the way Nancy loves Chris. She loves him in every way it's possible to care for a person. She knows his idiosyncracies, and this man and her children are the fabric of her life. Maybe one of the reasons we can make the audience care so much about us as people is because we care so much about each other.*

DON: *It's a good object lesson for the public to see a marriage that can weather the sorts of vicissitudes we have had to. It may be kind of corny, but I think it's a good symbol of what American life can be. We've taken pride in building a family, even though the family has had a lot of troubles. We show the things that have to go into keeping a family together—the love, compassion, tolerance, and understanding.*

HELEN: *But we've had our differences.*

DON: *Well, marriages have to have their crises. Nancy tends to have an emotional reaction to some people. If she doesn't like someone, she just doesn't like them. When we first went on the air, Nancy's son Don was engaged to a girl by the name of Janice Turner, and Nancy just didn't think she was good enough for her son. Don was a brilliant student, studying the law, and Nancy just didn't feel this girl had enough education of her own to be able to back up Don in his career. Janice married another man, had a couple of children, then divorced, and later when Don did marry her, Nancy cried all the way through the wedding. Nancy can be quite opinionated.*

"You have much more of a chance to show your responsibility as an actor in this medium. The scripts have often been written too quickly. The author may want something particular from a character, but he hasn't had enough time to think it through to make it work in the script, so the actor has to find the way to make it happen. If you have a long number of scenes year after year that are similar, you have to bring something to it that will make the audience pay attention." —DON MACLAUGHLIN

HELEN: *Whereas Chris is a lot more tolerant. He's out in the business world and he can't afford to indulge his emotional whims the way Nancy can.*

INTERVIEWER: *I read what you said about a woman, a friend of yours, who said she found it easier to talk to you as Nancy than as Helen.*

HELEN: *Yes, that's the mother of a friend of mine. No matter what I do she always talks to me as if I were Nancy. She's a very intelligent woman. I guess she's just come to feel that she knows Nancy so well from having watched her all these years that it's impossible for her to separate us.*

INTERVIEWER: *Has the town of Oakdale changed much over the years?*

Helen Wagner is back in her dressing room, all finished with her day portraying Nancy Hughes.

"Soap opera is basically character, not story. It's the people in it who make it work. I think we could coast along and do nothing really for two weeks and they'd say, what's the matter with those people, why aren't they doing anything? But they'd still watch. It's like the cave men telling a little story every night by the fire and then gathering the next night to hear a little more of it." —DON MACLAUGHLIN

DON: *I don't think so. Not any more than Plains, Georgia, or Webster, Ohio, where I was born, has changed. People grow up, move out, move back, get married, divorced, all that. The normal things. We haven't dealt with artificial insemination, the pill, and all those things that the other shows are getting into to try to mirror life in America. We're like the Waltons. We haven't dealt with cults or homosexuality. Not that there isn't homosexuality in every community, I suppose, but here in Oakdale, it just wouldn't seem right.*

HELEN: *The biggest change that happened came when we changed from a half hour to an hour. The way they split us up into a morning cast and an afternoon cast, you can't really know what's going on unless you read every script to find out.*

DON: *It's kind of sad the way we're all split up now. We used to all gather the previous day and read the show and discuss it and argue about it. You became involved. You heard the whole show. Now, we just do bits and pieces and we've kind of lost that ensemble feeling.*

HELEN: *Now it's taped. It was a much better show when it was live because it had more immediacy.*

DON: *I don't know whether the public knows it or not. Maybe that's our saving grace. But we know it.*

HELEN: *It's amazing when you stop to think about how long we've done this show.*

DON: *I get letters all the time, people saying they've watched it ever since the beginning, and you think, my gosh, since 1956. I sometimes wonder how many words it would be if you added up all the words we ever had to say.*

INTERVIEWER: *Do you sometimes feel as if you've each had two marriages—your real marriages and your soap opera marriages?*

HELEN: *No, because . . .* DON: *I love Helen very much, but . . .*

They hear that they've both spoken at once. They both stop at the same time, look at each other to go on, then laugh.

POSTSCRIPT

Down the hall, as they wait for the elevator to come, Eileen Fulton (who plays Lisa) joins them, and they talk over the schedule for cast photos. Don apparently missed

Nancy and Chris Hughes (Helen Wagner and John MacLaughlin) *have one of the few marriages in all of soapland that seems able to endure.*

the memo, so Helen fills him in on the details. They pass by the CBS security guards and step out onto the sidewalk. It's a sunny summer afternoon, and as they all stand for a moment to take in the welcome fresh air a black limousine pulls up and stop by the curb. Eileen climbs in the back seat as the chauffeur holds the door for her. The interviewer says goodbye. Don and Helen look at each other, nod in unspoken agreement, then turn to walk, arm in arm, to the corner where they'll catch the crosstown bus.

(L to r) Henderson Forsythe (Dr. David Stewart) and Don Hastings (Dr. Bob Hughes). "People who watch get involved not only for the story, but also for the characters. People care about what happens to the people in the story . . . well, really not so much what happens, but how it happens. How is my friend going to come out of this thing? You don't get much of it around New York, but when you get out of here and on the road, people treat you like an old friend. It's not that pawing kind of adoration that Paul Newman would get or you'd get if you were a big star. They come up and say, 'Gee, it's too bad you lost your wife.' Their questions are mostly about my character and about the family. 'How's Nancy? How's Chris?'" —DON HASTINGS

The everlasting Hughes kitchen with the cast of characters that have been there for years: Nancy Hughes (Helen Wagner), Bob Hughes (Don Hastings), and Chris Hughes (Don MacLaughlin).

John Dixon (Larry Bryggman) *and Kim, his wife at the time* (Kathryn Hays). *"John Dixon is probably from a family that wasn't very well off and so he had to struggle to get what he wanted in life. That's good soap material. But he's also very talented. He's good at what he does. He's a fine doctor. Yet he always wants something a little bit better. He wants to better his position. That's a natural thing, really. Everyone wants to do that, but we present it as if it were something evil to be ambitious."*
—LARRY BRYGGMAN

"I don't think of John Dixon as a bad person, I just think of him as someone who's got to do what he's got to do. I don't think of him as an 'evil person' even though I know the producers think of him in that way. I think they prefer to have black and white characters. The more of that, the better in soap opera. But I think it's a very depreciative view of the audience, the idea that unless things are drawn in huge, bold strokes the audience isn't going to get it. In essence it's saying that you're not good enough to understand so we have to put it on a cartoon level for you. It makes me mad when they write this sort of sweeping, stereotyped stuff simply because they like the 'going away scene' or the 'reunion scene' or the 'put-down' scene. They don't seem to care that much about character development. It's all ratings and numbers. If tomorrow it was proven that more people would watch this show if we all had humped backs, we'd all have humped backs. And if it was proven that viewers liked people with German accents better, we'd all be talking with German accents. The actors, the directors, and the people who are actually involved in putting the thing on try to create characters that make sense, but while you've got some people who are actually concerned with what they're doing, you've also got a bunch of people who care about nothing but the ratings."
—LARRY BRYGGMAN (John Dixon)

"I grew up in the Midwest and this town, Oakdale, is Midwestern too. People have lived here all their lives. They know the town and they love it. We don't get into what the town is really like that much—it's more this particular living room or that particular kitchen. It's upper-middle-class America, professional people, people without any money worries. We never talk about money or how much things cost. And it's basically a town of conservative values. The old virtues, the old truths, are important to people. And there are good people and bad people, though we don't have any really bad people. The eternal verities, the Ten Commandments, honesty, forthrightness, trustworthiness—that's what the overall storyline is all about. —HENDERSON FORSYTHE (David Stewart)

Bob Hughes (Don Hastings) *and Kim Stewart* (Kathryn Hays). *"Kim tends to show her strength more in moral courage than in animal courage. Sometimes the audience finds that annoying. They want her to stand up for herself and not let her own feelings go by the wayside in order to protect other people. I wish she could be stronger myself sometimes too. I thought it was wonderful when she decided to keep her baby and raise it by herself, but unfortunately that storyline wasn't carried through. There are a lot of women like myself who are single and who have children. I'd like to see them do more stories like that, to show what women go through in their life-styles now. Kim's not really the kind of woman who would just sit around. I'd like to see her have some kind of work. Many women now have families and carry their home responsibilities, their family responsibilities, and are responsible in business too."* —KATHRYN HAYS

Melinda Peterson (Pat Holland) *applies her make-up in her dressing room.*

Henderson Forsythe (David Stewart) *takes a moment out from rehearsal to rest and study his script.*

"*When the part of Lisa on* As the World Turns *was offered to me, I was told she was to be a temporary character, a mere foil for the young Bob Hughes, who had just entered college. The Lisa the writers had created was made of 'sugar and spice and everything nice.' I wanted the part. It would be a good break for me, but inwardly I was repelled by this character. She was me and I was sick of her. Sweetness and goodness had been shoved down my throat all my life and, at that time, I was rebelling against everything I had been taught. I was fighting for my identity. The producers, of course, had no way of knowing that my own world was spinning, colliding against tradition, my family, myself. So, at every opportunity to make her just the least bit conniving, I played it to the hilt. The writers saw that what I was doing worked. The girl who was to be written out in a few short weeks suddenly started getting more material, and I began to create the lovable monster she has become.*" —EILEEN FULTON *writing in* How My World Turns, *the story of her years working in soap opera.*

"On our show we're always involved in divorce, love, illegitimacy, blackmail—and it's all done over coffee. We've had stories where people are dying of a terrible disease. We can describe the disease, its symptoms, and everything. We can even draw you a picture of it. But we can't mention the disease. I had a storyline when my ex-wife and I were having a child. I was the traditional nervous father, and at one particular point I had some dialogue with the doctor about his deciding to use a fetal heart monitor, a device which apparently is used to measure the heartbeat of a child. They cut the dialogue. When I asked why, they said that they didn't want to alarm any pregnant women and they didn't want every pregnant woman who watches the show to demand that she get a fetal heart monitor. Nancy Hughes and I had a scene where we talked about the fetal heart monitor, and by the time they were done cutting the stuff out of it, it was 'Hello,' 'Hello,' 'How are you?' 'I've got to go.'" —LARRY BRYGGMAN (John Dixon)

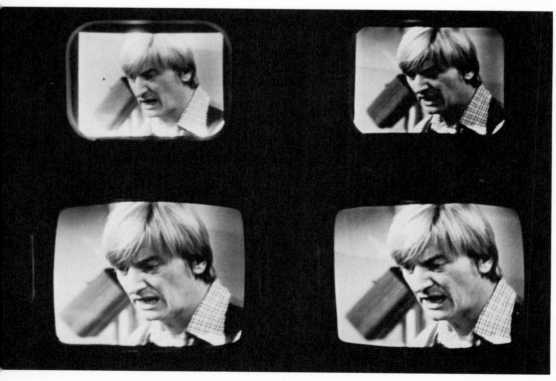

Larry Bryggman "on the air."

"When I came in Irna (Phillips) wanted to make Bob a doctor. So I went into medical school in September, and in October I was at work in a hospital. It was a quick education. No wonder I lose so many patients. Actually, there's a lot of Bob in me and a lot of me in Bob. You have to do it that way. You take what the writer creates and you round it out. Writers don't really have the time to round out the characters on soaps. They write a kind of general thing and the attitudes you as an actor play will lead them to write it that way. I may have a reaction to somebody in the story, and rather than say, 'Oh, really,' I may play a negative reaction that might then become a part of the story. A lot of big parts have been started on this show and never lasted, and yet guys who have come on to do small parts end up as stars of the story. Bob Hughes has become a person to many people. I have a friend who is a doctor and he tells me that I'm a better doctor than he is. He has great respect for me because he could not communicate with one of his patients, and one day when he walked in she was watching the show I was on and she told him, 'Now there's a real doctor.' I'm that kind of old-fashioned doctor that still makes house calls, that takes time with patients." —DON HASTINGS

After their scenes have been shot, actors often gather in the control room to watch the rest of the show on the monitors as it's taped. Here, Don Hastings (Bob Hughes) and James Douglass (Grant Colman) discuss what they see on screen.

Judith McConnell (Valerie Conway) *and Don Hastings* (Bob Hughes) *rehearse a scene together.*

from the script

ACT I

FADE IN:

HUGHES KITCHEN. DAY. AFTERNOON. CONTINUED FROM TUESDAY.

Nancy is alone in the kitchen and working on some kind of light summer dessert for tonight's dinner. In the middle of it, she stops and suddenly remembers something.

NANCY [TO HERSELF]: *I must get hold of Dee or Annie.* [SHE GOES TO THE SINK AND RINSES AND DRIES HER HANDS. SHE'S ABOUT TO CROSS TO THE PHONE WHEN DONALD ENTERS. HE WEARS A TIE, SUMMER SUIT, BUT HE'S CARRYING HIS JACKET]

DON: *Mom, I'm leaving.*

NANCY: *To see Dick Martin?*

DON: *Yes.*

NANCY: *Well, if you're going downtown in all this heat, I hope you feel as fresh and clean as you look, Donald.*

DON: *Last nights rain sure didn't help, did it?*

NANCY: *I think it's worse than before.*

DON: *It'll cool off soon—maybe by tonight.*

NANCY: *I hope so.* [SHE LOOKS AT HIM AND SMILES] *I must say you look a lot better than you did about an hour ago.*

DON: [GRINS] *I was kind of a mess, wasn't I?*

NANCY: *When you take her to the park—I can understand Franny getting dirty. . . .*

DON: *It was that double-dip ice cream cone. I thought she was old enough to handle it by herself. . . .*

NANCY: *Well, now you know.*

DON: [SMILES] *And helping her make those highways and tunnels in the sandbox didn't help either.*

NANCY: [SMILES] *I think you had a better time than she did.*

DON: [NODS] *Not bad.*

NANCY: *And you certainly tired her out. She didn't complain at all when I put her down for her nap.*

DON: *Good.* [HE SEES WHAT SHE'S BEEN MAKING AND CROSSES AND PERHAPS LICKS A SPOON OR SPATULA THAT'S BEEN IN A MIXING BOWL] *Hey, I remember this dessert! You making it for tonight?*

NANCY: *Yes.*

DON: *Terrific!*

NANCY: [CASUALLY] *Well, I hope it turns out. It won't have any strawberries in it this time.*

DON: *How come?*

NANCY: *I've heard Valerie Conway doesn't like them.*

DON: [LIGHTLY] *That's right—tonight's the big night, isn't it? The poor girl has to come and stand inspection.*

NANCY: [NOT THINKING IT'S FUNNY] *It won't be like that at all.*

DON: *Yes, I know—but I'm really looking forward to meeting her, aren't you?*

NANCY: [FLATLY] *I've already met her.*

DON: [AMUSED] *It must have been some meeting. You don't sound that happy about it.*

NANCY: [STANDING FIRM] *It was very quick. I doubt that we exchanged more than ten words.*

DON: [SENSING NANCY'S OBVIOUS RELUCTANCE AND TEASING HER] *Well, tonight you'll have a chance to sit down and really get acquainted.*

NANCY: [NOT THAT PLEASED AND UNABLE TO HIDE IT] *Yes—I suppose.*

DON: [LAUGHS] *Mom, you never change. You remind me of when Bob and I were teenagers and first starting to date.*

NANCY: [FROWNS] *What do you mean by that?*

DON: *Never mind. I think I'll quit while I'm ahead.* [LOOKS AT HIS WATCH] *Besides, I've got to go. I'll see you later.*

Rachel (Victoria Wyndham) *worries Dr. David Gilchrist* (David Ackroyd).

ANOTHER WORLD

IN THE EARLY SIXTIES there was a battle raging among the three television networks over who could capture and keep the lucrative daytime television audience. CBS always had a steady lead with its collection of dependably successful soaps. ABC had failed in a couple and after that didn't seem to make much more of a sustained effort. NBC did make an effort to compete, but being the "we try harder" soap makers, they were skittish and often took their shows off the air too soon, not allowing for the many years it can take to build up a loyal soap opera audience.

Then, simultaneously, both ABC and NBC entered the field with a new weapon—the hospital soap. Instead of a central family being the pillar around which all stories revolved, there would be a hospital with all the melodrama and intrigue of doctor-and-nurse relations and peculiar accidents and illnesses. ABC premiered *General Hospital*; NBC aired *The Doctors*. Both shows were highly successful. Then, as if riding the momentum of this new wave of soap success, NBC stole Irna Phillips away from CBS in 1964 and hired her to create a new show for them.

Irna used her old formula—character development and family travail—to create a show very similar to *As The World Turns*. But now she added a new slant. This new show, *Another World*, would grapple with high emotion and dramatic tension rather than ordinary day-to-day life. Each episode would open with an admonition: "We do not live in this world alone, but in a thousand other worlds . . . the events of our lives represent only the surface, and in our minds and feelings we live in many other hidden worlds."

Another World was located in Bay City. William

(L to r) *Steve Frame* (George Reinholt), *Rachel Matthews* (Robin Strasser), *Russ Matthews* (Sam Groom), *and Alice Matthews* (Jacqueline Courtney) *are out for dinner in Bay City. Russ and Rachel are married and Alice and Steve are dating, but unbeknownst to all but Rachel, Rachel is pregnant with Steve's baby.*

"Steven—oh, I liked him. I liked him a lot. He was a real man's man—a he-man type of guy. Real nice. He didn't have that long hair or a beard or anything. He kept himself real nice. And he always had money. He had his own business and so he always had lots of money to spend." —a fan

Matthews headed up the wealthy half of the Matthews clan; his brother, Jim, was patriarch of the poorer side of the family. The serial began with William's death, and the storylines initially developed out of its consequences. In one, his widow, Liz, became desperate in her efforts to cling to her two children, Bill and Susan. When Bill fell in love with a poor orphan girl named Missy Palmer, Liz made it her business to break up the affair, chasing Missy out of town and to Chicago, where the waif ended up embroiled in underworld business through the influence of a new boyfriend named Danny Fortunato. Soon she was implicated in Danny's murder, and only Bill's arrival in the nick of time got her off. The two married and moved to San Francisco to be as far away from possessive Liz as possible, but then Bill was killed in an accident and Missy was left a young widow.

Jim and Mary, the poorer Matthewses, had three children—Russ, Alice, and Pat—and their troubles long provided the focus of the stories in the show. When Pat was young, her boyfriend, Tom Baxter, got her pregnant. She had an abortion and was told that she wouldn't be able to have children as a result. The news upset her so much that she killed Tom. John Randolph was hired to defend her, and he succeeded both in getting her free of the charge and in making her his wife.

Meanwhile, Pat's brother, Russ, became a doctor and married a young woman named Rachel, who quickly proved her colors as the town bitch, going after every man in sight while her husband worked night and day at the hospital. One of them was Steven Frame, a wealthy, handsome, and not altogether trustworthy owner of Frame Enterprises. Both he and Rachel had grown up poor and shared a "from the other side of the tracks" view of the world. Though Steve had his sights set higher—on the cultured and demure Alice Matthews—he never seemed to be able to get troublemaking Rachel out of his mind.

Thus began a love triangle of huge proportions that was the main feature of life in Bay City for years

"Rachel was a bitch. I mean a real selfish brat. I don't know why. Her mother was nice enough but maybe it was because her father ran off when she was little. She used to run after every man, especially the married ones. She liked to have any man another woman had. When she went and broke Steve and Alice up, that made me so upset. She just couldn't wait to tell Alice she was carrying Steve's baby. I don't know what was wrong with that girl, I really don't." —a fan

Dear *Another World:*
 . . . And how can you possibly allow Steve Frame to use Rachel's own father against her? How can you allow him to lie about her that way. Steve and her father are the only two men that Rachel ever really loved. How can you hurt her this way by having the two of them turn against her? If she can stand this torture and survive she will have proved how strong a person she is. But why do you feel you have to put her through it? I just don't understand the point of such an unhappy story.

Dear *Another World:*
 As of yesterday, you lost one of your most faithful viewers. I just cannot take this unfair treatment of Rachel anymore. Good-bye.

Steven Frame was the founder and director of the prosperous Frame Enterprises.

Steve and Alice got married the first time around after Alice came back to Bay City to reveal the truth of Rachel's lies and conniving.

The second time around.

Rachel (Victoria Wyndham) *just couldn't get Steve Frame out of her mind, and she tried everything to try to get him to leave lovely Alice and return to her.*

Happiness didn't last long. Steve went off to work in Australia and on the way home his helicopter crashed and he died.

After Steve's death, Alice Frame went ahead with her plans to adopt a child, Sally (Cathy Greene), even though her Bay City friends protested that it would be a strain for Alice to raise the child alone.

and years. Rachel was brunette and bad; Alice was blonde and good. When Alice wouldn't give Steve all that he wanted, he naturally turned to Rachel, who naturally ended up pregnant, a fact she announced to Alice just as Steve had convinced her to marry him. Alice was so upset she ran away to Paris without giving Steve an explanation. Meanwhile, Rachel let husband Russ think the baby was his. When Alice returned from Paris and told Russ the truth, he sued for divorce. Steve and Alice got back together and got married for what would turn out to be the first of two separate times.

All was well in the marriage except that Steve made regular visits to his and Rachel's son, which brought him close to Rachel. Understandably, this dismayed Alice. She got pregnant to try to draw Steve's attention back home but ended up losing the baby. Meanwhile, Rachel's no-account father showed up in Bay City with a scheme that he thought would get him some of Steve Frame's money. He engineered a breakup between Alice and Steve by

arranging for Alice to come across Steve when he was alone with Rachel. Once again Alice disappeared from Bay City, and Steve, not understanding what had happened, finally decided to bow to Rachel's desires and divorce Alice to marry her.

When Alice returned to Bay City, once again the truth came out. Steve wanted to divorce Rachel so he could go back to Alice—he ended up breaking the law in his efforts to do it. He was sent to jail, and under the strain, fragile Alice had a mental breakdown and was sent off to a sanitarium. When Steve and Alice were both released, they got married

Rachel and Mac married. Everyone was pleased except his daughter, Iris, who was, after all, Rachel's same age.

When Rachel met Mackenzie Cory (Douglass Watson), a man nearly twice her age, it looked like she had finally found the secure love of a man.

On Mac's urging, Rachel took up sculpture as a hobby. When she showed talent, her hobby quickly blossomed into a full-scale career and posed a threat to the stability of her marriage to Mac.

again. Then Steve went off to Australia to look over business prospects and ended up getting killed in a helicopter crash.

The resolution of this historic soap triangle, Steve's sudden death, was the result of casting changes that were afoot behind the cameras at *Another World*. George Reinholt as Steve Frame and Jacquie Courtney as Alice were beloved by *Another World* fans, the most celebrated actors in all of daytime television. But both of them also had developed reputations for taking advantage of this enormous popularity by frequent outbursts on the set. A new writer and a new producer had taken over the show, and after working with this popular pair for some time, decided they would do better to produce the show without them.

The departure of Reinholt and Courtney from *Another World* was an historic event in the world of soap opera. Accusations were made on both sides. Press conferences were held and statements were released in which both parties stated their cases. The soap opera magazines attempted to mediate by giving both sides a forum for clarifying what had happened. From whatever perspective, however, it looked like the producer, Paul Rauch, was taking a huge risk with the show's ratings by canning its most cherished actors.

Reinholt moved swiftly and negotiated new roles for both himself and Jacquie Courtney on *One Life to Live* at ABC (he has since left). This was a soap that desperately needed a boost in ratings, and the producers must have been pleased to get the new actors, particularly since in many parts of the country *One Life to Live* was aired at the same time as *Another World*. In the end, *One Life* did see a boost in ratings, but *Another World* didn't suffer either. It began to top the Neilsen ratings on a regular basis and went on in 1976 to win the Emmy for the best-produced serial on daytime television.

Perhaps one underlying reason for the conflict, aside from the personality clashes that invaded their working relationship, was an underlying conflict between George Reinholt and writer Harding Lemay about the interpretation of the character of Steve Frame.

Steve had been Reinholt's creation. He didn't make up the character, but it was his own personality and acting style that had made the character as popular as he grew to be. Reinholt, like Steve Frame, had grown up poor and later became a big professional success. In playing the part, he certainly drew on his own background as a street kid from the slums of Philadelphia. He was particularly concerned with the problems of a poor person who tried to climb into a new economic class by associating with people, like

the Matthewses, of higher social standing. Reinholt explained, "Anyone who wants to come out of bad conditions to better ones isn't to be put down for wanting that. I came out of the gutter in South Philadelphia, and I would never want to live there again; it was the most tortured and unhappy period of my life. It's the climb up from the gutter to wherever it is that you think you should be that distorts, cripples and destroys. The whole modus operandi is to distract you with the material aspects of class into thinking you have improved yourself by moving from a cloth coat to a fur one. Steve Frame was living out an idealized state rather than living out who he was and what he really was feeling about himself."

When Harding Lemay took over writing *Another World*, he too identified with the character. He explained, "When I started writing the show the character of Steve didn't have his background clearly spelled out, so I gave him one pretty much like my own. I decided that he had run away from home like I had at seventeen, that he had lived on a farm and his family had been poor, and that many of his adult problems came from not having been properly understood when he was younger."

Both Lemay and Reinholt had a private and personal vision of the character and motivation of Steve Frame. Unfortunately, they did not coincide.

The end of this historic Bay City love triangle made way for other changes in the storyline of *Another World*. Rachel began to undergo a transformation from soapland's biggest bitch to a much more subdued and mature woman. This happened not long after actress Victoria Wyndham was hired to take over the part from Robin Strasser, the actress who had played Rachel for years. Writer Lemay explained that he didn't like his characters to be as black-and-white as was standard in the world of soap opera; he wanted to make Rachel a character with more complexities.

In the new storyline Rachel met and married Mackenzie Cory, an older, wealthy gentleman who gave her the love and security she needed to become a more likeable person. One development was that her hobby in sculpture blossomed into a full-scale career as a sculptress, and for a while, this created problems in their marriage. Mac was jealous, unable to handle the fact that he was no longer the focus of Rachel's life; Rachel didn't want to give up her new-found identity. The result was the very modern problem of a woman in a conflict between marriage and a career.

Another World is renowned in the soap opera business for having attracted some very famous and successful New York stage actors to its cast, most of whom continue to pursue their stage careers while acting their parts on TV. One reason is executive producer Paul Rauch's reputation for wanting top-notch actors and being willing to pay the price to get them. The result is a cast that has starred, among others, Jacqueline Brookes (Beatrice Gordon), Irene Dailey (Liz Matthews), Constance Ford (Ada McGowan), Hugh Marlowe (Jim Matthews), Anne Meacham (Louise Goddard), Dolph Sweet (Gil McGowan), and Douglass Watson (Mackenzie Cory).

Both Paul Rauch and Harding Lemay originally come from theater backgrounds, and together they have introduced more of traditional theater into their daytime show. Lemay ruled out old soap staples like amnesia and unmotivated melodramatic plots from his scripts, ended the long speeches that had typified soaps, and introduced dialogue that emphasized conflict between characters. Rauch and Lemay were also the first to expand their serial to an hour, beginning a trend that many others have since followed.

More recent storylines in Bay City have included the romantic entanglements of people connected to Frame Enterprises. At one point, Alice, deserted by her new husband, fell in love with her one-time brother-in-law, Willis Frame, who had proven himself to be even more untrustworthy than his brother Steven. Willis loved her back—but he also loved his longtime girlfriend, Angie. In the end he lost both of them. Meanwhile, Rachel's marriage to Mac Cory had been on rocky ground, threatened by the machinations of Mac's scheming and jealous daughter, Iris, who was furious that her father married a woman even younger than she.

Despite changes of characters, actors, writers, and producers, *Another World* still carries on in much the same spirit as Irna Phillips's early creation. This is still a soap specializing in highly stylized passions of love and romance, and it still represents the original incantation: ". . . the events of our lives represent only the surface, and in our minds and feelings we live in many other hidden worlds."

Dear Another World:
  Don't let Iris get rewarded for her lying, cheating, and manipulating. I knew an Iris once and that kind of woman deserves all the unhappiness she gets. My children come home from school to watch your show and I want them to see clearly that Irises of the world get their just deserts . . .

Dear Another World:
  Are Steve and Alice ever going to get back together again? The thing with Steve and Rachel and Alice is getting to be too much to sit through. Either get Steve and Alice together for good or I quit watching the show. A lot of my friends feel the way I do too. Watch out or your ratings are going to go way, way down. I love Another World, *but I can't stand by and watch Alice feel heartsick too much longer . . .*

Dear Another World:
  Why don't you just kill Rachel off! Everyone is sick of her and her troublemaking. . . . And why do you keep Alice acting like a baby? She has to start to face up to the things that are causing her problems, not run away from them all. The true Steve loves her very much. Does it make you happy to see the ratings of your show going down because you insist on keeping Alice and Steve apart? You have really made a mess of things by letting that repulsive little bitch, Rachel, run the whole show. My eight years of watching Another World *have gone right down the drain. There's really no point in watching anymore. For a while you had a wonderful show with two perfect people—Steve and Alice—together. Now that you've got Rachel right in the middle of it again, the whole thing is sickening. From now on I'm watching* General Hospital, *instead.*

Dear Another World:
  Rachel is the only reason I watch your show. Stop ruining her life. Stop it at once! Contrary to what you seem to think, there are plenty of us out here who like Rachel. Sure she's not all good like Alice, but Alice is unreal. Rachel is a more honest personality. No one else on the show can compare with her fighting spirit. She's right to fight to keep her husband and her son. A lot of us out here watching wish we had half the guts she has to stand up for her rights. She's not all bad. She had an unhappy childhood, but we like her. We like to see characters who have had a rough time. It makes them stronger people. Rachel fights back and good for her.!

A DAY IN
Another World

THE BUILDING looked more like an old armory or an abandoned post office than a television studio. It was brick, there were no windows, and the streets nearby were lined with drab coffee shops, five-and-dime stores, thrift shops, and garbage. I stood there bleary-eyed. I had gotten up at five-thirty in the morning to get out to Brooklyn by seven, the hour actors start arriving to spend their day in the NBC studios of *Another World*.

The cars began to pull up—an "East Side car," bringing actors in from the East Side of Manhattan, a "West Side car," bringing them from the West Side, a car from Westchester, and one from Connecticut. The actors emerged looking rumpled, drowsy, and rather unspectacular. Douglass Watson, winner of the New York Critics Circle Award, stepped out. He plays sophisticated and magnanimous Mac Cory. Then came Beverlee McKinsey, who plays Iris, Mac's wealthy daughter. There was Anne Meacham, the Cory maid Louise, who both on screen and off talks to her house plants and names them after mythological figures. There was Constance Ford (Ada McGowan), the unshakably maternal member both of the *Another World* cast and of Bay City. One by one they hit the curb, yawned, and climbed the steps into the studio. Then one more car pulled up. A chauffeur descended, circled the car, and opened the back door for Victoria Wyndham, *Another World's* leading lady. She stood on the sidewalk, brushed her long dark hair back and away from her face, and reached her arms ahead of her to stretch. She wore blue jeans and a Mexican blouse. The day's script was rolled up in one hand. She must have been trying to use the car time to learn her lines but had apparently fallen asleep instead. Now she squinted at the early-morning light, glancing up and down the street and at the sky taking a look at the sunlight before pushing past the glass doors and disappearing for the rest of the day into *Another World*.

Inside the studio, the director for the day, Melvin Bernhardt, was busy going over instructions with the technical crew, who had begun setting up lights and arranging the sets at six A.M. Bernhardt, one of three men who alternate directing responsibilities, had prepared for this day's shooting by making a blueprint that shows where the actors will stand on the set, when they will move, and how the cameras will be set up to shoot them.

The early-morning rehearsal in which the director first works with the actors is closed to outsiders, so I wandered around the empty set and watched stagehands and technicians quietly setting up lights and putting props in place. There were the offices that were the scenes of family in-fighting at Frame Enterprises. There was the Cory kitchen, and it was luxurious, a scene from *House and Garden*. But everything was quiet and empty and strangely two-dimensional. A man walked by carrying a vase of flowers in one hand, a cake box in the other, and a newspaper under his arm. The cake box went to the top of the refrigerator in the Cory kitchen, the flowers behind the couch in the Cory living room, the newspaper by the telephone. The three cameras on the set looked like large prehistoric animals. They were poised, motionless, but inside they were humming. TV cameras are never turned off because the cooling and heating is dangerous for their delicate electronic parts; they stay awake each night, keeping their own silent vigil over Bay City.

Soon people appeared on the set coming from all sides. Boom men climbed up to their seats above their cameras. The cameramen took their places. Bernhardt stepped out from between two stagewalls.

"We spend more time inside these brick walls making this show than we do inside our own homes." —PAUL RAUCH, EXECUTIVE PRODUCER

The Cory kitchen stands waiting.

David Ackroyd, who played Dr. David Gilchrist, collects his day's wardrobe in the early stages of morning preparations.

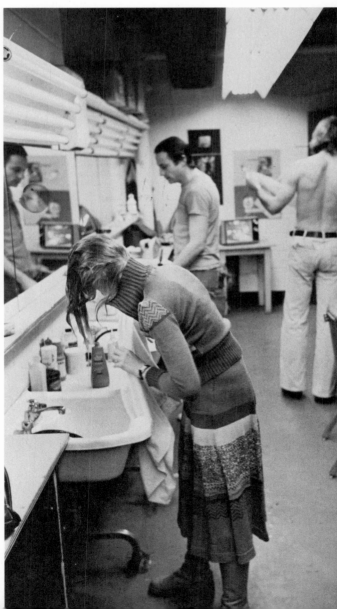

After blocking the day's scenes on the studio floor, actors and actresses file upstairs to the dressing rooms and makeup rooms where they wash their hair, have haircuts and styling, are made up, and sort out the costumes they will wear later in the day.

Laurie Heineman (Sharlene Matthews) *gets help with her make-up.*

Jacqueline Brookes, as Beatrice Gordon, and Ted Shackelford, as her son Raymond, run through a rehearsal of a scene in which they argue about Beatrice's meddling in the affairs of the Frame family.

The afternoon run-through gets under way after the director has had his meeting with the producers and when all the technical crews have arrived back from lunch.

Director Melvin Bernhardt directs cameraman Carl Eckert.

"All right, let's go. Let's get started. Where's Victoria Wyndham? Vicky?" He looked around the set. "Where the hell is Vicky?" From the opposite end of the studio a woman's voice called back, "I'm down here!"

Bernhardt consulted his script while he waited for her to take her place in the shot. "Move that coffee tray, someone, please. It doesn't belong in this setup." The man on camera one leaned out from behind the viewer. "I'm in tight on you in this shot, Vicky," he said softly so just she could hear. "Try not to move too much."

Bernhardt spun in place. "Who's on camera two? Camera two, they've got a lot of dialogue here. This is shot five. I want you to get a wide angle." Then he turned to Doug Watson, who was taking his place in the middle of the set. "You have to hit that spot exactly." He pointed to one of the stagehands. "Mark it for him." The stagehand moved forward, took two strips of masking tape, and marked the spot on the floor.

> Dear *Another World:*
>   I have watched the show since its beginnings, and I have always expressed myself on it. Here I go again: Do you think the young should have no morals? Molly is a little tramp! I used to like Mike until he got involved with her . . .

I sat perched on the Cory kitchen counter, which was on the set opposite where they were working. Everything was moving so quickly I could hardly follow what was going on. Then Bernhardt suddenly raised his arm, pointed in my direction, and an army of cameras, technicians, and sound equipment did an about-face and began moving across the floor straight toward me. "Scene four, Cory kitchen." I stepped free of the commotion just as Rolanda Mendels came from behind and plunked herself down into a chair at the kitchen table. Rolanda plays Molly Randolph, a promiscuous young lady who's in Bay City making up for time she lost as a country kid on the farm.

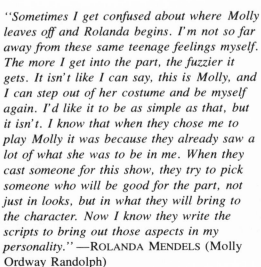

"Sometimes I get confused about where Molly leaves off and Rolanda begins. I'm not so far away from these same teenage feelings myself. The more I get into the part, the fuzzier it gets. It isn't like I can say, this is Molly, and I can step out of her costume and be myself again. I'd like it to be as simple as that, but it isn't. I know that when they chose me to play Molly it was because they already saw a lot of what she was to be in me. When they cast someone for this show, they try to pick someone who will be good for the part, not just in looks, but in what they will bring to the character. Now I know they write the scripts to bring out those aspects in my personality." —ROLANDA MENDELS (Molly Ordway Randolph)

"I like the character of Clarice because she has a genuine love of life. The character has always been fun. I came on as the 'tacky broad,' and it was wonderful because I had the fun of being the one who always said the wrong thing at the wrong time. The character has had more and more troubles lately. After I had my baby and was lying in the hospital bed, I looked up at the doctor and said, 'I used to have such a good time before I came to Bay City,' and he looked back and told me, 'Well, those are the wages of sin.'" —GAIL BROWN (Clarice Hobson McGowan)

Olive and John Randolph (Jennifer Leak and Michael Ryan). "I've been given a chance to portray a man's development through middle age and the crises that that age can bring with it. He's undergone a change as his children have grown up, and he loses some interest in his family and begins to look around at younger women. I think that's a drive in many successful men in middle age who want a way of proving themselves by proving that they can still be attractive to younger women. Very often this leads to the dissolution of the marriage, and then they wake up and realize, my God, what have I done! And eventually it leads to a new awakening. To me that's been an interesting aspect of the character. You only get to do this sort of thing on a soap opera where you can slowly watch the development of a character over time." —MICHAEL RYAN

"When they hired me they didn't have an exact idea of what the character would be. They watch me and what I'm doing with it, and over time that's how the direction of the character is decided. It does put me under a certain amount of pressure. In the first month I just didn't know where to go with it. I didn't know whether to make the character nice and warm or cold and high-powered. It wasn't a question of their not wanting to help me. They just weren't sure where they wanted to go with it yet." —DAN HAMILTON (Jeff Stone)

During the break I wandered upstairs through the cinder-block halls where the cast has its dressing rooms. Victoria Wyndham was busy washing her hair as her "mother," Constance Ford, talked with her about summer houses and children. Hugh Marlowe (Jim Matthews) had fallen asleep while going over the script in an easy chair in his dressing room, and Mike Hammett (Dennis Carrington) and Bobby Doran (Jaime Frame) were sitting on the steps at the end of the hall eating sandwiches out of waxed-paper wrappers.

Rolanda Mendels came up behind me. "You going to eat lunch?" She grabbed me by the arm. "I'm getting some yogurt. Come on. I've got to get out of here and see the daylight." On the street we passed Joseph Maher, who played the Cory's chauffeur. He was looking at second-hand furniture in a thrift store window, and as we talked a moment I had the peculiar feeling of being out on the street with imaginary little people who live inside TV sets.

Nothing ever stops during a day of production of *Another World*. Even while the camera and sound men were out on their lunch break, the producers and director had been meeting with the various people in charge of production to go over the day's work so far. Executive producer Paul Rauch had been watching the run-through on the closed-circuit television set in his office, and over the lunch break he and his producers discussed their reactions to what they had seen—everything from how the lighting looked to which lines they'd have to cut in order to fit into the time slot. After this meeting, Melvin Bernhardt hurried upstairs to the make-up room to meet with the actors for "notes." He tells them about changes in the script and criticizes how lines were read.

Just before three o'clock people began to gather back on the set for the dress rehearsal, and I was suddenly caught off guard. The actors looked strangely different, and it took me a minute to tell what the change was. All through the morning they had looked like ordinary people. They wore their own clothes—crumpled shirts and jeans, sneakers and sandals. They had ordinary human complexions with blotches, dark lines, and freckles. Now as they hurried to their places, they looked peculiarly clean and perfect. The men wore pressed suits. The women wore modest, matronly dresses. All hair was perfectly in place. Faces were perfectly toned. Dark circles and blemishes were gone. It seemed strange to me and even a bit eerie.

I took the place I had been assigned in the control booth. From dress rehearsal on, only actors, cameramen, and boom men are allowed on "the floor." Everyone else is in the control booth, and communication between actors and the director goes on through overhead speakers.

Bernhardt had the command seat in front of a bank of TV sets, flanked left and right by his technical staff and assistants. He was under pressure now: he snapped out instructions like a military man. The pressure broke one actress, who lost track of her lines and stopped to complain that the teleprompter was being held out of view.

Right after dress rehearsal, Bernhardt left to consult with the producers one more time. He returned with a list of problems: the cake box prop was being held like there was nothing in it, dialogue during one scene wasn't clear enough. Bernhardt was moving fast now. He returned to the control room and clamped on his head set. He was ready for the final tape.

The control room was silent and tense. All joking and wisecracking had stopped. Bernhardt watched the seconds tick off, his hand raised in the air, ready to cue the announcer. With a drop of the hand, the music began, and Rachel Cory, walked into her living room in Bay City.

At the end of the first act, there was a minute to breathe as the "black slug"—the one minute of blank time into which the network would later plug

Director Melvin Bernhardt meets with the day's cast on the set of Jim Matthews's parlor to give his "notes"—line changes, blocking changes, suggestions on changes in interpreting scenes, and general reactions to the day's acting performances thus far. Actors and actresses arrive for this final session with the director dressed in their costumes and ready for the final taping that is scheduled to begin at a quarter to five.

"It's an interesting thing. We've had four or five presidents and a couple of assasinations and Watergate and the wars, and through all this the show still goes on. It's kind of got a life of its own. It just goes on and on." —HUGH MARLOWE (Jim Matthews)

Producer Mary Bonner meets with the director and technical staff for "notes"—comments on the day's production up to that point and suggestions for changes to be made.

Final taping begins:

Ken (William Lyman) *fights with Mac* (Douglass Watson).

And Willis Frame (John Fitzpatrick) *demands an explanation from young Michael Randolph* (Lionel Johnston).

Jim Matthews (Hugh Marlowe) *puzzles Beatrice Gordon* (Jacqueline Brookes).

its commercial—was fed onto the tape. Even during the break, no one spoke. Bernhardt watched the clock tick off seconds. At five seconds before the end of the minute, his hand was raised in the air again. He dropped it. The action began.

Paul Rauch slipped into the side door of the control room and leaned up against the wall to watch the monitors. All through the day production had built up momentum from its first sleepy morning hours, moving ahead into the afternoon like a steamroller, building toward this moment. At the next "black slug" Rauch tapped Bernhardt on the shoulder and smiled. The people in the control room took note of this nod of approval, and there was an almost audible group sigh of relief.

As soon as the taping was done, actors and actresses went up to their dressing rooms, changed back into their street clothes, returned their costumes to the wardrobe room, and waited by the exit ready to go home, all done with a speed that seemed to defy human possibility. Then the word arrived: "The tapes have been cleared." The technicians had done a quick run-through to check for problems. There were none, and that was the signal that everyone was free to go.

> *Dear* Another World:
> *. . . I'd like to tell you what I think of Alice Frame. Now that you've got a new actress for that role she's become so sugary and naive it's sickening. I'm getting tired of her being so frail and dopey. I'd like to see her stand up on her own two feet and take a look at what's really going on around her. Willis pulls the wool over her eyes so easily and it's just not really believable. A woman like Alice who has had so much to go through in her past would never be so naive about the people around her . . .*

At six P.M., the actors filed back out the studio doors. They wore their street clothes now. Their faces looked ordinary again. They carried new scripts. They looked exhausted.

As I watched them, I thought of Alice walking back out through the looking glass. There was something strange about the transformation these people made from themselves to their characters to themselves again. That windowless brick fortress they spent their day in really was "another world." Twelve hours would pass and then they'd be back again—back through those glass doors, that looking glass, that led into their lives in Bay City.

The Mellowing of Rachel Cory

Victoria Wyndham plays Rachel Cory, the star character of Another World. Some years back when she was shopping in Bloomingdale's in New York, a woman came up to her, started hitting her, and shouted, "I hate you! I hate you!" The woman was finally restrained by the store guards, but at least she'd had her words with Rachel, the ruthless mischief-maker of Bay City. Such occurrences aren't uncommon for actresses who play soap opera villainesses, but they don't happen to Victoria Wyndham anymore. Below, Vicky discusses how the romance with Mackenzie Cory came about, and how it changed her from a bitch to a mature beauty.

Douglass Watson, who plays Mac, had been on the show for a while before I ever had a scene to play with him. Then one afternoon I went over to his house to pick up my son, who was playing with his grandson, and when I walked onto the scene, even though it wasn't written into the script, I just naturally flirted with him. And Mac, being who he was, just naturally flirted back.

When they saw the scene on tape, it made sense to everyone. It was an obvious thing. Here was a man who could give Rachel the security she never had. They hadn't planned for Mac and Rachel to fall in love, but they said, why not, maybe this is the direction we've been looking for.

They decided to try it even though they were concerned that the viewers might think it was tasteless for an older man to be interested in a younger woman. It was six months before we did anything physical. Doug and I both wanted to be sure there was no tackiness so we developed it slowly. By the time we did the first kiss, which we did in a restaurant, of all things, the audience was really ready for it. They wrote in to tell us that this was a totally different kind of relationship for Rachel and that it was something she really needed. Here was a man who was smarter than she, who was terribly sophisticated, who knew all the wiles of women, who could be a father figure to her and be someone she could finally open up to and talk to about her disappointments. The audience wrote telling me to marry him, and they wrote to the producers telling them not to break us up.

Mac was the one to suggest to Rachel that she take up a hobby after they got married, and though she fought it at first, when she did take up sculpture she began to develop as a person. Before, she had always felt that she couldn't be anybody unless she was married to somebody . . . now she was at last beginning to feel comfortable about being herself.

Rachel loves Mac. It's the security she's felt in her love for him that's enabled her to grow. She doesn't need him in the insecure way she once did; she can love him from her strengths rather than her weaknesses, which is what love really ought to be.

"Soaps are highly undervalued because people who flip on the soaps just once don't understand that the people who have been watching for years get twenty times more out of the show because they know all the history and the characters. If you brother walks into a room, for example, nothing much might be said between him and your mother, yet you know there's a lot going on there beneath the surface. It's not spoken, but it's hinted at. No other art form in the history of the world gives the development of characters this way going on over a number of years." —DOUGLASS WATSON (Mac Cory)

"The things that make Rachel feel threatened just aren't the same things that make me feel threatened. My life isn't like hers. I was brought up very securely. I had parents who loved me. I had financial security. Sure, I'm volatile like Rachel, but in a different way and for different reasons. The things that send Rachel up the wall wouldn't matter to me a bit. What people think in the town? That doesn't bother me. The Matthewses could do their whole number and it wouldn't make me mad." —VICTORIA WYNDHAM

"When they brought me on to play the part I told them that I didn't want to play just a heavy. I was willing to play an anti-social character. There's lots of room for examining that kind of person. But I told them I would only play it if it was motivated and if there was room for her to grow. When they hired me they said that's exactly what they wanted her to do, and they told me that if I ever found that they weren't letting her grow I could quit." —VICTORIA WYNDHAM

When the writer was looking for a hobby to give Rachel, Victoria Wyndham came up with the idea of sculpture. A sculptress in her own private life, she promised to provide the pieces they would need in the storyline of the show.

"Rachel Cory and Victoria Wyndham are two different people. The only way that my life as Vicky affects Rachel is through the ideas that go into Rachel. For example, I wouldn't have been able to play the mother aspect of Rachel if I wasn't a mother myself. I wouldn't be able to play someone who does sculpture and is just discovering that she has a career in her if I didn't know what a career meant to a woman who's been taking care of children. I know what it means to go back to a career after you've thought of yourself as just a housewife." —VICTORIA WYNDHAM

Soap Opera Writers: "In the Beginning Was the Word . . ."

"Actors in soaps identify very strongly with the characters they play. Concurrently with their own life they're living another life. They never play the same scene twice so it's really like living another person's existence. They'll say to me, 'I know this character better than you do and she wouldn't do that . . .' When I was new to writing the show, I was in the control booth one day and the actress reading one of the tag lines must have known I was there because she read it and then looked straight into the camera and said, 'Yeah, and whatever that means.' It takes a soap writer awhile to prove himself. I think of soaps as a marvelous form about day-to-day human relationships. Writing a play you deal with the highlights of a life, but in soaps you're dealing with everyday lives. That's what soaps should be about, showing ordinary people dealing with the problems of daily life." —HARDING LEMAY

Soap opera writers are a species unto themselves. They create life in mythical towns and for mythical families. They establish justice, mete out punishment, and arrange that everyone gets his just deserts. Soap writing takes a special temperament and a special talent. Scripts have to be turned out every day without fail, and a good soap writer knows how to pace himself, conserve his strength, and produce no matter what his mood or inclination.

Headwriters are the kingpins in the field, and each has his group of assistants or dialogue writers. Among the latter, usually one, sometimes two, become the headwriter's protegé, and eventually, after an apprenticeship according to time-honored conventions, the soap writing mantle gets passed on like a kind of inheritance. For example, Wisner Washam, now primarily responsible for All My Children, *was trained by its headwriter and creator, Agnes Nixon, who was herself trained by Irna Phillips.*

But sometimes there is a break with convention, and someone outside the known circles of television soap operas is brought on to be a headwriter on a show. One writer to come in through this unorthodox route is Harding Lemay, the current writer of Another World.

Lemay had written many stage plays, but he'd done hardly anything for television when producer Paul Rauch read his autobiography, phoned him, and said, "Your life has been a soap. How would you like to write one?"

"I never really thought I'd take the job," recalled Lemay. "Writing soap operas was about the last thing I had in mind. But I was broke and I thought I should at least go talk with them." He prepared for his meeting with Procter & Gamble, owners of Another World, by spending three weeks watching soap operas and taking notes. "There were four different shows that had courtroom trials running at the same time. They bored the hell out of me, and I figured if it was going to bore me it would bore an audience even more. They'd rely on melodrama instead of real human drama. They'd superimpose some catastrophe, like giving Althea on The Doctors her fourth brain operation in four years. They all had these crazy stories about amnesia and nurses getting pregnant because they didn't know about birth control.

"I didn't know Procter & Gamble owned some of these other shows too, and I sat in the meeting with them blithely tearing the shows apart. They just looked at me and let me go on and on. God knows how I ever got the job."

When Lemay was hired Irna Phillips was brought in to teach him the tricks of the trade. She showed him her "three-burner method" for writing soap opera based on a metaphor about cooking: the story reaching its climax was on the front burner, on the middle burner was the story building up to a peak, and on the back burner was the story just beginning. You just moved the stories around like pots; when the front burner was all done, you took it off, moved the other pots up, and got something new cooking on the back.

Harding Lemay grew up in upstate New York (not far from

where his mother had been raised on an Indian reservation) on a poor farm where his parents struggled to eke out a living to feed their family of thirteen children. Today, when he introduces new characters to Bay City that have recently come from the farm, he relies on his own background to describe them. In fact, "Most of Another World reflects what I have experienced in my life. The very rich people like Iris Carrington are based on the wealthy people I met when I worked in publishing. Through them I experienced the careless cruelty of the very, very rich people who are used to always having their own way. And the Frame family, those sister-brother fights, that's something I grew up with at home. Writing is a way of finding out more about the people you already know. It's a way of examining them. For example, Pat and John Randolph are very much like my wife and me. We never had the marital problems they did, but in dealing with their children, there's a similarity."

At five-thirty each morning he's at work at his desk piecing together the lives of the people of Bay City. Clipped to the music stand in front of him is the script for the day that's been prepared from his original outline by one of his sub-writers; to his right he keeps the original outline. Using both, he types up a revised version. By the end of Act III his household has begun to stir, and he joins them for breakfast before his brother arrives at nine to begin taking phone calls and retyping the scripts. After breakfast Lemay sits down to do Acts IV, V, and VI. "By then it's easy. The first six pages of the script are the really hard part. That's where you have to set the tone. Afterwards everything else follows."

A soap opera writer has to keep in mind more than characters and stories. Another World has over thirty-five regular cast members, and each has a contract specifying the number of days per season he must be used. It's the writer's responsibility to keep track of all this and juggle storylines in terms of contracts in order to keep within the alloted budgets.

With the day's script done, Lemay answers the messages that have piled up. He rarely goes out to the studio: if there's a question it has to be dealt with by phone. Calls come in: "How come you sent Willis off two weeks ago on business to Washington, D.C., and now you have him coming back from Baltimore?" "Vicky has a question about the tag line you gave Rachel." "Connie Ford has a play; you're going to have to write her out for three weeks."

A soap story is the result of many factors—the writer's own ideas, the influence of those who actually own the show and are concerned that storylines attract an audience, the opinions of viewers who write in, and the personalities and acting inclinations of the people who play the parts.

When Harding Lemay sits down in front of the television at three to watch the show, he allows no interruptions. He has that day's script in hand and he takes notes, jotting down the ideas that come to him as he watches his written material turned into images on the screen. One actor is consistently flubbing lines, but he's a good actor and Lemay wants to keep him on, so he writes a reminder to himself to keep that actor's speeches short. He notices too that actors he had planned to involve in a romance don't seem to hit it off on screen, and he makes a note to reconsider the planned storyline there.

Like Lemay, most successful writers are very attentive to the performances they see on screen, and most tend to write to the lead of what the actor gives to the part. William Bell, headwriter of The Young and the Restless writes only three weeks ahead of the air dates so he can retain the flexibility to change the story according to what he sees performed. A soap writer initially sets it all in motion, but then as the characters he's created emerge and the actors settle into their roles, his job is to guide them along in a story that they almost write themselves. Victoria Wyndham said of Harding Lemay, "He works like good novelists apparently do; he lets the characters write themselves. He goes with them rather than being autocratic about making them go where he thinks they should go."

An attitude of responsibility and seriousness about the task at hand is a canon of the business of writing soaps. The writers know they have huge audiences, and most take this as a commandment to be accurate and responsible about the information they present through the stories. Some use soap stories as an explicit arena for adult education, such as the natural-childbirth lessons and films shown on Ryan's Hope. In quite a few shows real-life organizations have been introduced so viewers know whom to contact if they need help with a similar problem. One Life to Live, for instance filmed episodes in Odyssey House, a drug treatment center in New York City. And Search for Tomorrow reenacted Alcoholics Anonymous meetings with careful attention to accuracy.

Harding Lemay is one soap writer who rejects the idea of "relevancy" in soap opera, but he does have a set of guidelines, if unspoken, that indicate his sense of responsibility to his audience.

"When a storyline was suggested that would have portrayed a social worker in a bad light, I fought against it," he recalled. "I told them I didn't care if there were only two hundred people out there who needed help from social workers, I didn't want a storyline that would go along with the cliché that the social worker is your enemy. We changed it so that she was an endearing lady with two kids of her own. I don't care if it was real or not. At least some person who needs help out there wouldn't be turned off to the idea of a social worker.

"Soaps do have an effect on people's lives. I got a letter from a woman thanking me for the Iris-Rachel-Mac story. She said it had helped her in her own life because she too had had a father who married a woman younger than herself and she had hated that woman for years. She said that in watching our story about the conflict between Iris and Rachel, she came to see that her father had a right to marry whomever he wanted. Every once in a while you get a letter like that."

He then added, "I don't expect to be doing this my whole life, but you know, a playwright hungers to see his work performed. The commercial theater is so demeaning the way it is right now. You can have an option on a play for eight months and have all sorts of meetings with directors and then nothing at all happens. With soap opera your work is put before an audience on a regular basis. I don't think any playwright works for any other reason than to watch his work performed." Harding Lemay feels some measure of satisfaction now; over seven million people watch his work every day.

Days of Our Lives

"Like SANDS THROUGH the hourglass, so are the days of our lives. . . . " On screen the sands of an ancient hourglass slowly shift balance as the comforting, fatherly voiceover of Macdonald Carey introduces the next hour of *The Days of Our Lives*, days that pass in Salem, where the troubled Horton family appeared on television in 1965 to usher in a new era in soaps. All the old soapland ingredients were there—a stable central family; sincere middle-class professionals; a Middle-American town; a preoccupation with love, marriage, divorce, and family life—but William Bell, who wrote the show, added glamour, wit, and signs of a more modern world. There was a lady psychiatrist, much

talk about psychological problems, a black family as regular cast characters, up-tempo bars and restaurants, and dialogue that was more realistic, more modern, and that even—until then considered a soapy sacrilege—included a bit of well-placed sarcasm.

If the characters on *As the World Turns* are appealing because of a nostalgic remembrance of things past, the people on *Days of Our Lives* are fun to watch because they could be your own family and friends. The Hortons behave like a real American contemporary family. Alice Horton doesn't spend her time sitting around the coffee pot, and she and her husband, Tom, seem to have a fairly resigned attitude about how much they can really influence the lives of their children. They seem to see their biggest contribution as providing a stable home to come back to when things fall apart.

After years of star-crossed love, Julie finally becomes Mrs. Doug Williams.

(L to r) Julie Banning (Susan Seaforth), *Doug Williams* (Bill Hayes), *and Addie Williams* (Patricia Barry). *When Doug Williams came to Salem, Julie took an immediate liking to him because she was getting bored with her marriage to Scott. Doug was after Julie's money because he wanted to open a new nightclub, and when he found out Julie's mother, Addie, was a more direct route to the cash he needed, he courted her instead. Julie was jealous, but Addie and Doug went off and eloped.*

Days of Our Lives came as a response to the popularity of the hospital soap. Writer William Bell combined the new hospital soap idea with the old and long-standing tradition of centering a serial around a family by making the Hortons a family of doctors.

The story of *Days of Our Lives* features Tom, chief of Internal Medicine at University Hospital, and Alice as the wise older couple overseeing four generations of Hortons. Originally, they had five children in the story—Addie, Tommy, Mickey, Bill, and Marie. Tommy was reported missing in action in Korea (he returned many years later); Addie died;

Mickey and Bill shared both a wife and a son; and Marie had an unhappy love affair early in the story and became a nun.

Salem is a cut above your average soap opera town. People are wealthier and a touch more sophisticated. Instead of congregating around the kitchen table or in someone's living room, Salem folks often gather at Doug's Place (the local hotspot) to gossip, romance, dance, and drink an unending supply of martinis. Even the local mental hospital is an indication of modern times. It's not the old "sanitarium" of earlier soap days where the mentally deranged would be sent off and not heard from again until they were cured. In Salem we see the daily workings of the mental hospital and are party to the ins and outs of treatment.

Along with storylines that show people in realistic psychological troubles, *Days of Our Lives* also offers rather heavy, and sometimes heavy-handed, doses of romance. The six-year on-again, off-again romance of Doug and Julie stands in soap opera history as one of the most drawn-out and titillating love affairs ever conceived and brought to the screen.

In the best tradition of celluloid romance, handsome, debonaire Doug Williams arrived on the scene in Salem as a mysterious stranger certain to cause a stir. He was an out-of-work nightclub singer and his ambition in life was to have a nightclub of his own.

Julie, granddaughter of Alice and Tom, fell for this new man-about-town as a distraction from her rather boring marriage to Scott Banning. Doug, hearing of the young lady's connections to wealth, obliged. But then he heard about her mother, who was single and a more direct route to the needed financial backing. He dropped Julie and went for Addie. And Addie, trying to discourage her daughter from breaking up a good marriage, got involved with Doug to keep him away from Julie. Addie eventually married him and bought him Doug's Place as a present.

Shortly afterward, Scott Banning was killed in a construction accident. Although Julie was still interested in Doug, he had developed a geniune love for Addie. They were expecting a baby when it was discovered that Addie had leukemia. She recovered

Scott Banning died shortly after Addie and Doug married, leaving Julie a lonely widow.

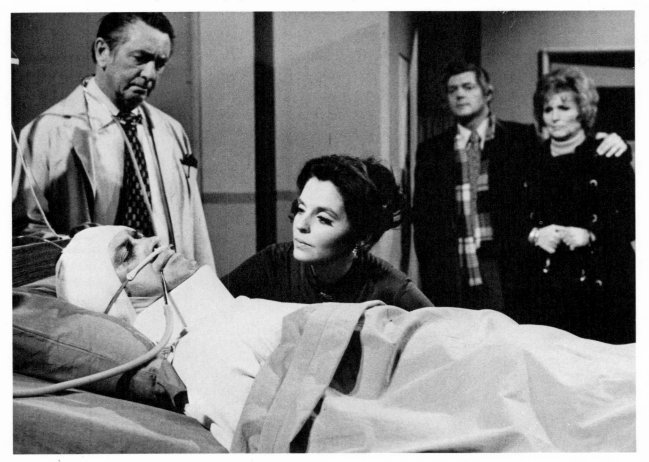

and the baby was born, but Addie was killed a short time later while trying to save her new baby daughter from a speeding car. Julie, however, was unavailable because in the interim she'd married Bob Anderson. Up and down the seesaw went. Everyone knew Doug and Julie were destined to get together, but somehow, to the vast disappointment of seven million anxious viewers, it just never seemed to happen.

Meanwhile, off-stage, Susan Seaforth, the actress who plays Julie, and Bill Hayes, the actor portraying Doug, began to develop a romance of their own. At first it was publicized by the soapmill as "just friends," but slowly it developed into a full-scale love affair. One weekend, unannounced except to a few friends, Susan and Bill got married. This set off a commotion among fans, who wrote endless letters to the show asking that the couple also be allowed to get married in the story. If they could get married in real life, so the argument went, they certainly should be able to get together on screen.

The writers and producers resisted the popular pressure, naturally milking the romantic tension for

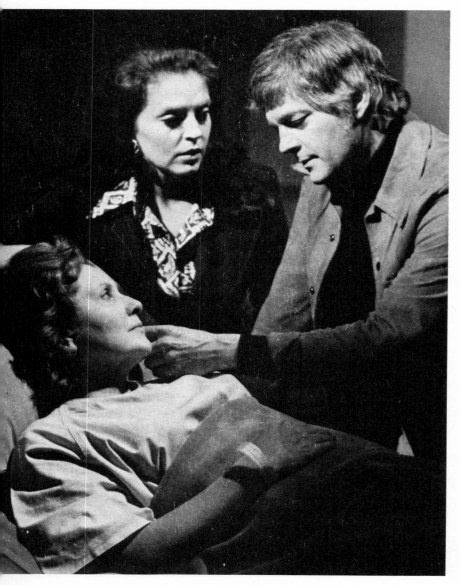

Later Addie died after saving her child from an oncoming truck and getting hit herself. This occurred not long after Addie recovered from a battle with leukemia, and viewers wrote into the show protesting her being killed in a way that they thought unfair. Betty Corday, executive producer, explained the reasoning behind Addie's death this way: "It's really very simple. We were not going to let Addie die of leukemia as many people suggested we should. I just couldn't do that to the viewers who are cancer patients or who have lost loved ones because of cancer when any day now doctors might come up with a cure for the disease. It just wouldn't be fair. I could not let the show say that the disease is hopeless, because there is hope. My husband died of a disease that today would be curable. There is always hope. But Addie's function in the story was at an end. It was always planned that she should die, but we wanted to find a means that was as quiet and dispassionate as possible. We just could not let her go through an excruciating death-bed thing, so it had to be quick. In the end she carried through her philosophy of being ready to sacrifice herself for her child, and she left life with all her joys paramount. It broke my heart to lose Patricia from the show. I love her as a person and have the greatest respect for her an as actress. But of course she's not the first actress to 'die' on the show, and the story must always come first."

After Addie's death it looked like Julie and Doug might finally get together, but more often than not they quarreled, and it took years and Doug's near death to finally bring the couple together.

Bill Horton (Edward Mallory) *and Mickey Horton* (John Clarke) *have been locked in sibling rivalry ever since Bill's girlfriend Laura* (Susan Flannery) *ended up marrying his brother Mickey.*

Young Michael Horton (Stuart Lee) is comforted by his mother and his "Uncle" Bill after Bill has just performed surgery to try to save Michael's "father's" life.

For many years Mickey Horton never knew that Michael (John Amour) actually wasn't his son at all, but had been fathered by his own brother Bill one fateful night when Bill raped Laura.

After recovering from surgery Mickey Horton suffered a case of amnesia and wandered away from Salem to a distant farmhouse where he met Maggie (Suzanne Rogers) and later married her. During this time Mickey took on the name Marty Hansen.

Back in Salem, with no word from the missing Mickey, Laura and Bill, whose love had been rekindled through the troubles they had shared together, decided at last to be married.

When Mickey returned to Salem and found out the truth about his brother being the real father of the boy he thought to be his own son, Mickey went off in a rage and attempted to kill Bill. He shot Bill in the arm, went into immediate shock after attempting to murder his brother, and was confined to a mental hospital where he slowly recovered his sanity.

all the audience devotion it was worth. Nothing was ever such a guarantee of good ratings as star-crossed lovers everyone knew belonged together. But finally the producers set the date for the marriage and *Days* put on one of the most extravagant weddings imaginable on the screen. It was such a soap opera media event that the local L.A. press (*Days*, along with *General Hospital* and *The Young and the Restless*, is produced in Los Angeles) was invited to the studio to watch.

Along with romantic fantasy, *Days of Our Lives* specializes in family tragedy. The tale of Horton brothers Bill and Mickey is nearly Homeric in its dimensions. It's a story of the tricky wiles of fate, so intricate in their ramifications that it's a soap story par excellence, exactly the sort of "long-arc" storyline that soap companies always aim for. It is also typically soapy in that it tells of an initial transgression by a character that develops into a moral tale requiring years before finally bringing it to justice.

Bill fell in love with Laura while they were both interns at University Hospital. She was studying to be a psychiatrist; he was studying to be a surgeon. Then Bill found out there was something wrong with his hands that meant he wouldn't ever be able to operate.

The Grant Family—(l to r) Danny Grant (Michael Dwight-Smith), *Valerie Grant* (Tina Andrews), *Helen Grant* (Kitty Lester), *and Paul Grant* (Lawrence Cook)—*made up one of the first black families to be regular cast members on a soap opera. Paul Grant worked at Bob Anderson's plant, and when David Banning* (Richard Guthrie) *moved out of his own home and boarded temporarily with the Grant family, he fell in love with the daughter, Valerie.*

David and Valerie caused a minor uproar in Salem when they announced their plans to marry. The wedding never took place, however, and David married Trish Clayton, who was pregnant with his child.

In anguish, he ran away from Salem, leaving Laura alone behind. She then turned to Bill's brother, Mickey, and by the time Bill showed up again, Laura and Mickey were married. Bill, heartbroken, responded by burying himself in his work at the hospital. This meant he worked late nights, and one night when both he and Laura were working, he went after her and raped her.

Laura got pregnant, and she knew the baby had to be Bill's because even though Mickey didn't know it yet, tests that had been taken indicated that he was sterile. Bill and Laura decided to keep this a secret and let Mickey think the baby was his. When the baby was born, he was named Michael, after his supposed father.

All through Michael's upbringing Laura and Bill kept their secret, but they also grew closer and began to fall in love again. Mickey, suspecting Laura of being unfaithful even though she actually wasn't, went off and had an affair with his secretary and decided to ask Laura for a divorce.

When Michael found out about his mother's supposed affair with Bill and his father's real one with his secretary, he had such a terrible fight with Mickey

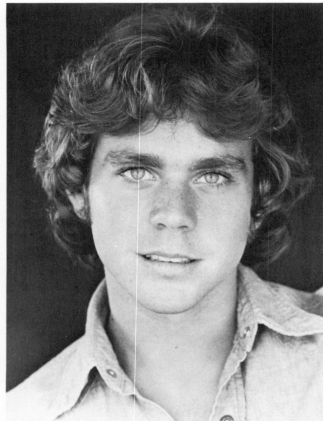

Don Craig (Jed Allen) is the debonair lawyer of Salem who nearly succeeded in marrying beautiful Julie before she finally settled down with Doug. His broken heart mended when he fell in love with Dr. Marlena Evans, Salem's second female psychiatrist.

Wesley Eure is the most recent actor to play the part of Michael Horton.

Rosemary Forsythe is the fourth actress to have played the part of Laura Horton, wife of both Mickey and Bill Horton.

that Mickey suffered a heart attack and landed in the hospital, where his life was miraculously saved by Bill.

The story went on: Though Mickey recovered, he was so depressed he suffered amnesia and wandered away from Salem. He assumed an alias, ended up at a farmhouse, and fell in love with a new woman. His family eventually found him and brought him back to Salem, where he regained his memory. It was then that he found out the truth about the real father of his "son," and he went into a rage and tried to kill his brother. This landed him in the mental hospital, where a long and slow recovery took place under the watchful eye of his psychiatrist ex-wife. Meanwhile, Bill had settled down happily with Laura and the two had another child. But Michael, now knowing the truth and filled with righteous indignation about the events of his family life, was still so enraged at his mother for her relationship with Bill that he refused to see the new baby for a long time or accept the marriage.

This Bill-Laura-Mickey story, abounding with nearly biblical messages of covetousness, adultery, and weaknesses of the flesh, is a perfect example of soap morality. The original transgression was Bill's for raping his brother's wife. Yet Laura was somewhat to blame too for turning to Mickey instead of being patient enough to wait out the return of her true love. Thus Laura suffered for her lack of faith by having to be married to the wrong man, and Bill was left out in the cold until he earned redemption for his bad behavior by saving his brother's life.

In more recent years, the story has featured an interracial love affair between Julie's son, David, and Valerie Grant, daughter of the show's black family. Both the Grants and Julie had misgivings

---

"Our ratings were on a very slow slide. At our peak we were riding up around the mid-thirties. Now they're mid-twenties, which by daytime standards isn't too bad, but it is down in that range which is considered the danger point. Once you get down there, if the network is looking to make a change for some reason, you're going to be the one they think about bumping."

—a soap producer

"In a sense we rely on a certain kind of ambiguity in telling the storyline. If you spelled everything out every day, people wouldn't be curious about what was going to happen. You hear this a lot from the people who follow the shows. They try to figure out where the story's going and they'll do anything to try and pry it out of you. We keep audiences involved in the story as much by what we don't say as by what is said."

—a soap producer

---

about the match, and the scripts included some very frank talk about the various racial attitudes.

Another "relevant" topic was wife-beating, complete with a therapy group for abused wives. The wife-beater, Fred Barton, received retribution in the form of a fall down a flight of stairs that left him paralyzed.

Julie and Doug have had their troubles too. Disaster befell Doug's Place when their liquor license was suddenly revoked, and Julie, in an effort to find a way to get it reinstated, went to see a shady rival nightclub owner who was in love with her to ask for his help. She ended up getting raped by him and then falsely accused of his subsequent murder.

And so it goes on, the hourglass turning and filling to pass the video hour in Salem as the Horton family, a true soap dynasty, carries on in a pattern of romance, transgression, and redemption through the unending days of our lives.

Doug & Julie
&
Bill & Susan

"LET'S MAKE EVERY effort to avoid each other as much as possible," says glamorous, if somewhat caustic, Julie Anderson.

"Well, I'm all for that," responds Julie's on-again, off-again lover, Doug Williams.

"We can start by your not following Don Craig and me wherever we happen to go!"

"Kim and I won't be caught dead here or anywhere in your vicinity," Doug assures her, his hostility rekindled by his injured pride. Julie has been announcing to all of Salem that she'll be marrying Don and leaving Doug in the lurch. Doug, meanwhile, has re-established a relationship with his ex-wife, Kim, and announced that they too will tie, or retie, the knot. "I guess it had to end this way," bemuses Doug. "Nothing maudlin, no shaking hands, no bidding each other Godspeed."

"Well, personally," Julie says, smiling between clenched teeth, "I can't stand the sight of you."

"Well," Doug obliges, "you don't look so good to me either."

Doug and Julie, soap opera's most star-crossed lovers, seemed likely to once again pass in the night and embark on marriages to other people. But within two weeks the story took an unexpected turn. Doug was hurt in a car crash, and Julie rushed to his side in the hospital. The accident shocked them to their senses, and there, among catheters and intravenous tubes, they finally agreed to marry. All of soapland breathed a great and contented sigh.

Bill and Susan Seaforth Hayes as Doug and Julie are probably the most expensive, to say nothing of the most successful, video-date couple in the world. Video-date services usually require that participants pay $100 each before they're recorded on tape to be shown to other date-a-maters. Susan and Bill didn't have to pay $100, but they did have Corday Productions's casting department working on their behalf. They were looking for a boyfriend for Julie, and they tested countless male actors on tape until they discovered Bill Hayes. Bill and Susan seemed a likely couple. There was the proper "chemistry." It shouldn't have been much of a surprise when the couple fell in love for real.

"We became personal friends while the characters were having an affair with each other," Susan recalls as she sits next to her husband in the commissary of NBC's Burbank, California, studios. Her hair is in curlers; it's midday and still hours from dress rehearsal. Bill's face is strangely pale because only half of his make-up has been applied. In the background, TV stars are lined up at the cafeteria looking as distracted and hungry as ordinary mortals.

"We weren't dating each other, but gradually we sort of slipped into it," Susan continues. "My mother had warned me years before—she was an actress and I've been in the business since I was four—that one of the basic tenets is not to get involved with the people you play with. My mother used to drum into me that actors are nearly the lowest form of human life."

Bill and Susan have been up since five in the morning and at work on the set since six. Here in the NBC commissary, there's no stand-up piano, no dry martinis, no softly playing music as in Doug's Place. It's just cheese omelets and saltines. Bill orders Susan a second glass of milk.

"When we started working together neither of us was at all interested in getting involved with anybody new," he says. "Susan was already seeing someone and I had just gone through a difficult divorce. But through those couple of years when the characters

"Lack of privacy is part of our business. We're on an hour network show, and that means we're in people's homes an awful lot. They come to know our faces, the sound of our voices. You just have to trade in privacy when you do a show like this. It's part of it. Usually people are nice. Most people who just come up and talk to you are nice about it, but there are some whose reaction is a bit irritating—the ones who say, 'You better give me your autograph, cause I watch you every damned day.' They think they own you. A lot of our fans are embracers and grabbers and huggers. Older ladies particularly have a tendency toward that. They come up and grab you on the street and when you try to get away they pull you right back. At the airport the other day a lady grabbed my head, my whole head. She said, 'Julie, Julie, it's so good to see you.' She shook Bill's hand and then turned around and grabbed me by the head." —SUSAN SEAFORTH HAYES

were carrying on their affair together we had lots of love scenes to do—and you have to rehearse them, then you've got to play them, and well, it got us pretty close. We were just good friends for a long time, but then—well, it did turn out to be a pretty good piece of casting."

On the set earlier that morning I had watched the two of them at work. They each went their own way, busy with make-up, reading through lines, consulting with the director and other actors. Once in a while Bill would stop near Susan, take her hand, and stand with her for a moment. Or Susan would come up to Bill and put her arms around his waist or across his shoulders. Sometimes she would stare at him from a distance as if, like her character Julie in the show, Susan just wasn't used to having a successful

relationship with a man. When they were on stage together, playing their parts, the switch to their screen roles appeared effortless.

The romance between Susan and Bill is the kind of story that soap opera fan magazines thrive on. While they were dating, one magazine called them up and offered to "give them a cover" if they'd hurry up and get married. "Then they called us up after the wedding," Susan recalls. "They said, 'Gee, why didn't you tell us ahead of time? We could have made a great layout on it.'"

Even after their wedding the couple was pressured by people who wanted to make their marriage a publicity event. "We had a friend who's a photographer at NBC who did the wedding photos for us. Afterwards there was a charming hoopla about who

Susan Seaforth and Bill Hayes celebrate their real-life wedding.

owned the photos, NBC or us.'' Susan laughs a little disheartenedly, then adds, ''Sometimes I feel I ought to tell people that no matter what it looks like, it was our own idea to get married.''

There have been other soapy couples: Peter Simon and Courtney Sherman (Scott and Kathy Phillips on *Search for Tomorrow*); Fran Meyers and Roger Newman (Peggy Fletcher and Ken Norris on *The Guiding Light*); and Stephanie Braxton and Dan Hamilton, who met on *The Secret Storm* and married while they were on *All My Children*.

But it was Susan and Bill whom *Time* Magazine called ''Soap's Hottest Lovers'' when they made them the cover for a feature article on soap opera. By choosing Susan and Bill, *Time* in its inimitable way, captured the very essence of the soap phenomenon: the fact that soap opera is about ordinary life and merges fact and fiction in a subtle way that is com-

forting and reassuring to viewers. When Susan Seaforth and Bill Hayes quietly went off in real life and consummated a relationship that had been created by casting departments, story writers, fans, and the actors themselves, they achieved the crowning moment of soap opera.

A rushed weekend to Las Vegas was all they got for a honeymoon, however, so after a few years of marriage they decided to take a three-week trip to Italy. When they told their producers of their plan to take a second honeymoon, the writers had to create a storyline that would allow the two actors to be absent from the set for three weeks. The writers' solution? It finally sparked their decision to bow to fans' requests and let Doug and Julie get married on the show. The Salem wedding was held on a Thursday. On Friday, the newlyweds left for their honeymoon. On Saturday, all four of them set sail for Rome.

Doug & Julie's Wedding Album

Doug and Julie's long-awaited on-screen wedding. (L to r) Brooke Bundy (Rebecca North), Suzanne Rogers (Maggie Hanson), Rosemary Forsyth (Dr. Laura Horton), Mary Frann (Amanda Howard), Susan Seaforth Hayes (Julia Anderson), Bill Hayes (Doug Williams), Robert Clary (Robert Le Claire), Edward Mallory (Dr. Bill Horton), Peter Brown (Dr. Greg Peters), John Lupton (Tom Horton, Jr.), Richard Guthrie (David Banning).

Macdonald Carey/Dr. Tom

After making over fifty films during his thirty-year stint in show business, Macdonald Carey settled down in 1965 to play the head of the clan in the new daytime serial called Days of Our Lives. He's since won an Emmy for the part of Dr. Tom Horton.

In the following interview his insights into the work of an actor and the meaning of soap opera provide that same seasoned vantage point he conveys in his role. The interview was conducted in Chadney's Restaurant opposite NBC studios in Burbank, California. Musak played at a discreet volume against the jingle of glasses and quiet murmuring of anonymous couples talking in corner booths. The seats were red vinyl and the waitress wore a mini-skirt. We had just come from Doug's Place, the restaurant/bar set on Days of Our Lives, and sitting down in the circular booth next to Macdonald Carey, it was as if we were still on the set.

QUESTION: Being a soap opera actor is generally considered second-rate in your business. How come someone like you with so many screen credits took a job on a soap?

CAREY: It was simple. At that time in the early sixties there wasn't that much work available. I have a lot of children to support and a lot of alimony to pay. When I was offered the job of the star on this show I said, sure, why not, and I took it. Strangely enough, it's turned out to be very rewarding in many other ways besides the money. There's tremendous security involved, and I've found that I have also learned a lot. In film I had gotten into a rut by taking my time with everything and not really learning my lines completely from the beginning. Suddenly I had to learn lines and perform them immediately. With a stock company, which is what we have on a soap, you have the security of not only knowing the people you're working with, but also the character you play. You grow into your character and develop it as you go along until it becomes second nature to you.

Doing the show has also been rewarding from the point of view of gaining recognition. More than the movies certainly more than the theater, soaps allow you to go anywhere and be recognized. You get a better table when you go into a restaurant. People are a little nicer to you because they know you and they know your character. The real bonus, though, is that you begin to get other jobs. When I first got into this my fellow actors said that I was demeaning myself. I overhead some people on the Laugh In show, which was across the hall from us, saying, "Well, that's the last refuge of the untalented." Nowadays actors who wouldn't have dreamed of it before are hammering at the gates to get in to do soaps. The whole point in this particular business I'm in—the acting business—is that you have to keep your instrument oiled, not only well-oiled, but used. And that's the great thing about soap opera—it keeps you working.

QUESTION: Why has there been such a stigma attached to soap opera acting?

CAREY: I don't think the level of the scripts used to be as high as they are now. The production values weren't as good and the whole tenor of the soaps and the language that was used in them was cloying and mundane. Long ago there used to be something called the Red Path Circuit which traveled through the Midwest playing in tents. The shows they'd do were so square and everything was completely black-and-white, no grays or any other shades. That's what soap opera was like. Now shadings have come into these daytime shows and the writing has improved. It wasn't just a question of getting better actors, because an actor is an actor.

QUESTION: I understand that a family feeling develops among the casts on some soap operas.

Heads of the clan: Alice (Frances Reid) *and Tom Horton* (Macdonald Carey) *look after four generations of Hortons.*

CAREY: Days of Our Lives *is like a second family you come to each morning. We come in in the morning and we re-establish ourselves immediately, reaffirm our links. If anyone is bad or bitchy or anything else, like in a family they get stepped on or laughed at or knocked around a bit.*

QUESTION: *I'm curious about what you once said about soap operas being "modern morality plays"—*

CAREY: *They are. That's their great attraction. It's like what the early movies used to be. Good always triumphs, the evil are punished, there's always a moral to be found. That's why people watch them, identify with them, and become so involved. It's like the current religious revival. Soaps fall right into this. For a whole segment of the society, soaps are the same kind of religious experience as TM or est or Hari Krishna. That's because you have two things. You have the identification with characters—people watch and say, well,*

that would never happen to me, but then they think again and realize it has happened to them, and to their neighbor, and to their friend. But you also get an uplift because at the same time you're identifying you also see evil being punished and good triumphing. The uplift is the moral lesson. That's exactly what the old morality plays used to do. The good man always wins. Adultery is punished. Thievery. Covetousness.

QUESTION: *How about the theme of the rich family always being neurotic and the poor or middle-class family always being full of love?*

CAREY: *The ruination of man by material things. . . . Morality means that people are punished if they do something wrong—if they go against the Ten Commandments. In soap opera, the person who transgresses suffers or is punished in some way. You see, that's the other meaning of the "soap" in soap opera. It's a cleansing thing. Soap opera—it's the soul's detergent.*

The two "father figures" of the set consult. Macdonald Carey (Dr. Tom Horton) and Wes Kenny, Days of Our Lives producer, meet outside Mac's dressing room door.

Wes Kenny discusses the interpretation of one of her scenes with actress Suzanne Rogers, who plays Maggie Horton.

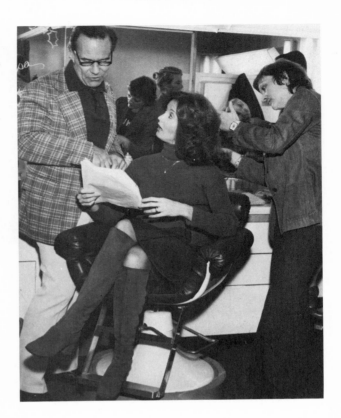

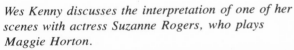

"In daytime it isn't just a question of how good your show is. You could come on the air with Gone with the Wind in twenty-six episodes and it would still take time to get a good rating. You have to break down the watching habits of women, and that isn't easy. I may be watching a terrible show, but if I've been watching it for five years, I have an inherent interest. I know the characters, I know the story. I can miss it for five days and still come back and know where I am. It may not be that good but an interest in those people has been built up over time. You hear a lot of philosophizing about what's good and what's bad and what creates interest and all about people developing a loyalty to a specific character, but what really happens is that over the years a show builds up its own audience. We built our audience over the first seven years because we came in and did things that hadn't been done before. We had more sex, and nice sex, not vulgar sex. We had Julie and Doug, and it was fun. We gained our audience, a large and loyal audience, and that's what the networks love." —WES KENNY, executive producer

Soap Opera Acting

Soap opera acting is a peculiar profession. Some say that it's very demanding work and some of the best acting being done in the country. Others say that it's the worst waste of talent and the most dependable method available to destroy an actor's natural skills. Some actors stay away from soaps; others won't do anything else, preferring the security of a regular job to the potential high status in another medium. For many actors who do soaps, though, and particularly the younger ones, it's a way to get started in a highly competitive profession. Most who start in soaps hope to move on. Others use soap opera acting as a way to subsidize their less lucrative theater work.

Soap opera actors work under contracts that specify a minimum number of days they are to be used. If they aren't used that much, they are paid anyway. If they're used more, they're paid accordingly. Regular cast members get upwards of $35,000 a year. Big-time stars like Mary Stuart earn between $100,000 and $200,000. Susan Seaforth Hayes and Bill Hayes each make over $75,000.

Many actors doing soaps hope it will pay off by helping them get nighttime television or movie jobs. But they also know that if they stay on a soap too long, they'll get classified as a "daytime actor," associated with the stigma of soaps, and may have a hard time moving on.

Quite a few actors who have become famous as TV and film stars got their start on soaps. Lee Grant, Don Knotts, James Coco, and William Redfield all did stints on Search for Tomorrow. Gloria de Haven played on As the World Turns. Andrea Marcovicci got her start on Love Is a Many Splendored Thing. Warren Beatty, Peter Falk, and Martin Balsam did parts on Love of Life.

For many soap actors, one of the big benefits of their work is that they are part of a repertory company, an ongoing group of actors who play together from week to week, who get to know each other as friends and colleagues. Actors who play regular parts often spend more time with their "soap families" than they do with their real ones. They celebrate birthdays together, gripe together, look after each other's welfare, and attend each other's weddings. In a notoriously insecure profession, the "soap family," for better or for worse, gives actors some ongoing security.

But soap opera actors work hard. Those who do the hour-long shows often wake to alarms set for four and five in the morning. Regular cast members usually do two to four shows a week, and central figures like Mary Stuart sometimes work all five days. There's a new script to learn each day, and for the hour soaps the scripts can run over sixty pages. Then there's the necessity to be able to take direction quickly. Most shows are read, rehearsed, blocked, dress-rehearsed, and taped in the course of one day. Once the actor is told where to stand and when to move, he has to commit it to memory and hit his "marks" exactly or he won't even show up on screen. Actors also have to be prepared to shorten lines, add lines, slow down, or speed up the delivery of lines—even if a cue to do so is given in the middle of the final taping—in order to make a show fit into a precisely timed television slot.

Soap scripts are written quickly, and even the top script writers sometimes turn up duds. Perhaps more than in any kind of acting, soap actors are in charge of their own characters. If the script is bad, it's up to them to add the sub-text or small changes in speech that can make it work. On some shows, particularly the ones with weak ratings, writers come and go so fast that the actor usually knows much more about his character—its history, motivations, involvements—than the writer does.

Sometimes soap opera actors become very protective of their characters. Conflicts between actors and writers develop, and it's up to the producer to mediate. Conflicts also develop when an actor feels he isn't being included in the main storyline often enough. When a character isn't in the main storyline, he gets the thankless task of "recapping"—carrying on boring conversations with other characters recalling what has been going on in the story that a viewer might have missed.

Soap opera actors are like long-distance runners who run alongside of themselves watching themselves run. Many have trouble at first getting used to a part that never ends. On the other hand, sometimes the end comes too quickly. Even when a character is going to be "killed off," the actor who plays the part often doesn't know it until he reads it himself in the script. This means that actors are rarely prepared for their demise, either as characters or members of the cast.

Sometimes the line between fact and fiction gets fuzzy in soap opera acting. Many soap actors switch easily over into the first person when talking about their characters. "Of course I tried to stop that marriage! I just didn't approve of the girl. . . ." or "Well, I have hurt some people, it's true, but you've got to remember I had a very unhappy childhood. . . ." Soap actors routinely deny any confusion between their soap characters and themselves, yet sometimes, particularly in the long-running parts, there are striking similarities in the two personalities. Outwardly, the lifestyle, clothes, and daily activities may be different; but inside there is something the same—a similar outlook on life, similar values, similar attitudes or personal conflicts.

Once an actor has a soap role, he usually has a lot of freedom to determine the character's direction by how he plays his scenes. Actors and actresses who have been playing parts for a long time often settle into a comfortable style of playing their characters that inevitably draws heavily on their own personalities. Playing a part day in and day out for years, through all kinds of problems and every manner of emotion, an actor inevitably has to draw on many different aspects of himself. When acting in a theater production, an actor takes on a personna for a short period of time and then drops it. When acting on a soap opera, a long-running actor often settles in for a life.

All soap operas that have been on the air for some years make a habit of celebrating the show's birthdays. When Days of Our Lives *marked its tenth year on the air, they calculated how far they had come in some other areas as well: in 2558 shows, they had performed 1,230,000 lines, rehearsed for 28,000 hours, shot 1200 miles of tape, and consumed 1,230,000 cups of coffee.*

All My Children

ALL MY CHILDREN made its debut in 1970 with the promise that it was going to be something new in the world of soap opera—a socially relevant soap that would deal with contemporary issues. Another imaginary town would go on the map, but this time, breaking with soap convention, viewers were given an idea of its exact locale. Pine Valley was just an hour's train ride from New York City.

Pine Valley would soon come to stand for all that's good in American life, a sort of soapy apple pie emphasizing the intimacy of small-town life. New York, at the other end of the train ride, would represent the temptations and confusions of the troubling

"Phoebe Tyler is awful but she's also loving. She really does think she knows best, and she is desparately trying to steer her children the way she thinks they should go. —RUTH WARRICK (Phoebe Tyler)

outside world. So, despite its commitment to face hard news eye-to-eye, *All My Children* was still at heart a soap opera that looked backward, exalting small town isolation in nearly religious terms.

Agnes Nixon created and wrote *All My Children*. She announced her desire to be a writer shortly after graduating from college. Her father, who didn't like the idea, arranged a meeting for her with "a professional writer," assuming that Agnes would be respectfully humbled and sent home where she belonged. The professional writer turned out to be Irna Phillips, who, far from discouraging her, hired her immediately to begin writing dialogue for *Woman in White*. That began a career that has made Agnes Nixon one of the most financially successful writers in the soap opera business.

She spent her first six months with Irna Phillips in Chicago, writing dialogue and learning the trade.

Then she moved out to New York and on her own, eventually taking over the writing of shows like *The Guiding Light*.

It was in the early days of writing *Guiding Light* that Agnes first demonstrated her penchant for introducing controversial and educational topics into her storylines. After a close personal friend died of uterine cancer, she wrote a storyline which had Bert Bauer, head of the Bauer clan, go off to the doctor for her first vaginal exam in years. Bert's tests showed early symptoms of a problem, which gave the doctor (and Agnes Nixon) the opportunity to give the TV audience a stern lecture on the importance of Pap smear tests. This was in 1965, when such subjects weren't discussed on television, and both Procter & Gamble and CBS registered objections. Though they wouldn't allow the use of words in the script like "cancer," "uterus," and "hysterectomy," Agnes persisted in her own quiet but forceful way, weaving around the banned words and keeping the plot moving along for six months until the entire lesson was learned. For her efforts, viewers wrote in to thank her; more than one had discovered early symptoms in time to get treatment.

All My Children was nearly stillborn as a soap opera. The initial scripts and all the plot outlines were lost in a suitcase. When they reappeared, Procter & Gamble, after initially optioning a new soap, decided they didn't want it. The scripts went into the drawer along with Agnes's hopes of moving up the soap ladder from headwriter into the more lucrative and prestigious position of soap opera creator.

Then she was given *Another World* to take over from Irna Phillips, who had created it but hadn't managed to bring in high ratings. Agnes invented the Rachel-Steve-Alice triangle that turned *Another World* into a huge success. Now ABC approached her to create a new show for them. Rather than digging out the old *All My Children* proposal, she developed a new soap, *One Life to Live*. When that was a success, ABC wanted another. This time she did return to that drawer, and *All My Children* has turned out to be one of the most popular shows in daytime.

It quickly met its promise to introduce social issues into the story. Mary Fickett, in the part of Nurse Ruth Martin, got one of the very first Emmys ever awarded to daytime TV for an episode in which she made a moving speech protesting the Vietnam War. Agnes had introduced a Vietnam War story into the plot by having one of the main characters, Philip Brent, drafted and sent to Vietnam. Back home, he was listed as missing in action, but the story showed him being taken in by a Vietnamese family in the jungle and growing close to them as they nursed him to health. This was a very novel and typically soap opera approach to the issue of war. Rather than taking an ideologically political stand, Agnes Nixon presented the issues by creating compassion and understanding for the people involved—an individual soldier and a Vietnam family. These episodes were filmed on the banks of the Connecticut River, some miles north of ABC studios in New York. A set was constructed like a Vietnam village, and Vietnamese actors were hired to play the parts.

In an article in "The Journal of the Academy of Television Arts and Sciences," Agnes Nixon said, "We had the first legal abortion on television. We have dealt dramatically with the subject of male infertility. . . . We have had an eight-month campaign to educate viewers—particularly the young ones—to the endemic proportions of venereal disease and all its ramifications.''

For a story on child abuse, the show worked in cooperation with a Philadelphia-based group called CAPE—Child Abuse Prevention Effort. When episodes were aired in that area, a banner was run on the screen giving viewers a number they could call if they needed help with a problem.

According to *All My Children* producer Bud Kloss, ''We've been dealing with topics that nighttime TV never heard of. The reason we can treat subjects like this in soap opera is because from the beginning daytime was considered primarily a woman's medium, and these were topics that women were used to discussing.''

In addition to its reputation for relevancy, *All My Children* is also considered the ''college soap.'' Nobody knows just how many college students are actually watching, but they're obviously out there in great numbers. At the deKalb campus of Northern Illinois University, for example, a Chicago *Sun Times* reporter was told, ''This is the biggest thing happening here. I guarantee that two out of every three students on this campus can tell you the plot.'' And a group of Boston students organized a petition, complete with three pages of signatures, asking that one of their favorite characters not be ''killed off'' on the show.

Why this particular appeal to college students? Well, on a rather mundane level, *All My Children*,

---

Who's Who? by Mary Fickett

Who is Mary Fickett and who is Ruth Martin? After eight years of continuous performing I'm no longer quite sure how to tell them apart. What a question to answer—exactly the sort of question I did not need to face at the moment, as my daughter, Bronwyn, has just called to tell me in the midst of my rehearsal that an older girl in school had hit her on the head with a volleyball by accident and she was in the school nurse's office with an earache. And not reaching me at home, the dentist's office has just tracked me down at the studio to tell me that my son, Kenyon, had six cavities despite fluoride treatments. And I couldn't find the one key I had to my dressing room door, which meant that once again the kind gentlemen among the crew would have to go off in search of "Mary's key" under all the prop furniture pillows.

Such is the life and thereby the personality of one Mary Fickett. Very different from Ruth Martin—well, yes and no. Mary tends to run instead of walk, but so does Ruth. Mary tends to cope, and so does Ruth. Mary tends to cry—and goodness knows, so does Ruth. Mary tries to be honest with herself, I believe, and so does her character, Ruth.

When I was asked by Agnes Nixon to portray Ruth, I read the description of the character. She was a nurse. I faint at the sight of blood. She lived in a small town. I have lived all my life in New York City and its close environs. She had a teenaged son. My two children were then nine months and three and a half years. She had a sister. I'm an only child. She was a "good" person. Me—no comment!

But Agnes watches performers in her shows and she begins to write more of their own personalities into the scripts.

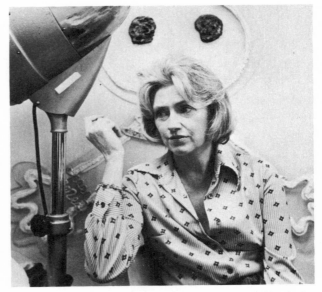

Over the years, as Agnes and I have become close friends, I have found that often a way I have of expressing myself begins to appear in the scripts. A gesture I have used unconsciously will be suggested in a script further down the line. She will even change her plots according to what she sees in a performer as she watches his work. If you are a performer on daytime drama—a continuous performer, not just one who comes on the program for a limited period of time—who you are as a performer and who you are as yourself get very intertwined. There is no question that I was what they call "accurate" casting for the part.

Kate Martin's living room.

Mona Kane's living room.

Mona Kane's office.

The nurses' station at Pine Valley's hospital.

(L to r) Bud Kloss, producer, and Felicia Behr, associate producer. "It's really sort of an X-ray machine, the TV. It tells you what the personality is like of the person who is on the other side. We cast that way. We cast toward the personality of the actor. Family feeling is what we try to project, in the story and in the cast as well." —BUD KLOSS

like *The Young and the Restless,* the other show particularly popular among college students, airs at the lunch hour when students are available to sit in student unions eating their bag lunches and following the plot. Another reason is probably the relevancy of topics and the opportunity to see some of the real problems that are affecting their lives dramatized. But a third reason is that *All My Children* has always specialized in love tangles of young people.

For years the mainstay of the storyline was a love triangle between the characters of Phil, Tara, and Chuck. Tara, the daughter of widower Dr. Joe Martin, and Phil, thought to be the son of Ruth, were high school sweethearts in the most thoroughly American style of teenage romance. Enter Erica, Pine Valley's brunette troublemaker, who had found out that Phil was actually the son of Ruth's sister, Amy. Erica spilled the beans, and Phil was so shocked at the news that he ran away from Pine Valley.

Tara, confused and disgruntled, turned her affections to Phil's best friend, Chuck, of the wealthy Tyler family. A new romance blossomed, but just as

One of soap opera's sturdiest marriages. Dr. Joe Martin (Ray MacDonnell) *and his wife, Nurse Ruth Martin* (Mary Fickett), *faced a challenge to their longevity when Ruth temporarily fell for young David Thornton.*

Once lovers, Brooke English (Julia Barr) *and Benny Sago* (Larry Fleischman) *are now "friendly" adversaries. Brooke, a spoiled little rich girl, stops at nothing to get what she wants. Benny, once a ne'er-do-well who was on his way to becoming soap opera's own Fonzi, has developed into a sympathetic character.*

High-handed, devious Phoebe Tyler (Ruth Warrick) *once used Benny Sago* (Larry Fleischman), *her chauffeur, to carry out some of her many intrigues.*

Benny (Larry Fleischman) *and Brooke* (Julia Barr) *in one of their many friendly debates.*

When actress Francesca James got tired of playing a character that was depressed all the time, she approached writer Agnes Nixon and asked if a change was possible. Agnes complied. She sent the character, Kitty Shae Davis, to a therapist, got her a new apartment and a job, and slowly a more positive outlook on life took shape. She was happily married to Linc Tyler, with everything to live for, when she died. This was not the end of Francesca James, however. She returned to the show some months later, with a new hairdo, as Kitty's long-lost twin sister, Kelly.

The star-crossed lovers of the older generation: Mona Kane (Frances Heflin) and *Dr. Charles Tyler (Hugh Franklin).*

The romance between doctors David Thorton (Paul Gleason) *and Christina Karras* (Robin Strasser) *fizzled when his wife showed up wanting him back. While attempting to kill the troublesome Edna, he accidentally killed himself.*

Chuck and Tara were to be married, Chuck collapsed at the altar with a kidney disease. In the meantime, Phil had returned to Pine Valley, and while Chuck was in the hospital recovering, the old romantic feelings between Phil and Tara began to be rekindled.

Then, suddenly, Phil received his draft notice and was called up. In a moment of high romance, Phil and Tara went off to a small church in the middle of the night, as a snow storm raged around them, and privately exchanged a secret marriage vow.

Phil and Tara consummated the "marriage." Some months later, when Phil was reported missing in action, Tara, now pregnant, turned to Chuck and accepted his proposal of marriage again. Assuming his father dead, they named the baby "little Philip."

When Philip senior eventually returned alive and well from the war, he drowned his troubles by turning to Erica, though he still loved Tara. She ended up pregnant, so he married her. Erica later had a miscar-

riage, and they were eventually divorced.

The truth about little Philip's paternity came out when he became ill and needed a blood transfusion; the matching blood types finally let Phil know the baby was his. After much agonizing, Tara and Chuck divorced and Tara married Phil.

The triangle, modified and expanded, continued. Little Philip, who didn't know Phil was his real father, wouldn't accept the new marriage and kept going to Chuck. This situation kept bringing Tara and Chuck together, much to the sorrow of Phil. Though Chuck was now married to Donna, he still had feelings for Tara . . . and Tara, meanwhile, was facing disillusionment in her marriage because of the demands made by Phil's job as a policeman.

Other than a commitment to young love and keeping up with the headlines, *All My Children* has all the features of a standard soap opera. There's the hospital, a rich setting for romantic intrigue and catastrophe. There's Nurse Ruth Martin, the classic soap

The new baby has finally been put to sleep and so Ann Martin (Judith Barcroft) *and her husband, Paul* (William Mooney), *take the opportunity for a family argument. In real life actress Judith Barcroft is married to* All My Children *scriptwriter Wisner Washam. Their son Ian appeared as little Philip in Pine Valley until the character underwent that speedy aging process that soap opera children sometimes face when the character is needed for a more mature storyline.*

(L to r) Tara (Karen Gorney), *Dr. Franklin Grant* (John Danelle), *and Dr. Chuck Tyler* (Richard Van Vleet). *Tara and Chuck grew up together, and when Tara's childhood sweetheart and secret "husband," Phil Brent, was reported missing in action in Vietnam, Tara turned to Phil's best friend Chuck so that the child she was about to have would have a father. Then Phil showed up back from battle. A messy triangle, and not a bad guy in the bunch.*

Hugh Franklin (Dr. Charles Tyler) *and Ray MacDonnell* (Dr. Joe Martin).

Director Del Hughes explains to William Mooney (Paul Martin) *and Robin Strasser* (Dr. Christina Karras) *how he thinks the scene should go.*

Director Henry Kaplan works with All My Children *actors during the "notes" session between rehearsal and final taping.*

Richard Van Vleet (Dr. Chuck Tyler).

opera "good woman" who never tires of listening to other people's problems and putting their welfare above hers. There's Erica Kane, bitch extraordinaire. And there's uppity, wealthy, and alcoholic Phoebe Tyler, whose brash intolerance is a constant test of patience to her family and friends in Pine Valley.

The wiles and prejudices of Phoebe are a constant source of good plotline. Originally she was married to Charles Tyler, a stately and considerate gentleman and Pine Valley's leading physician. Phoebe was fanatical about her intentions that her children, Ann and Lincoln, grow up and marry people of their same social standing. Both children rightly disappointed her.

Ann's first marriage was to the dashing but low-life dance instructor and saloon proprietor, Nick Davis. Although her second was slightly more suitable—to attorney Paul Martin—it resulted in a collosal mental breakdown following the crib death of their baby daughter.

Lincoln, meanwhile married Amy, who later was discovered to have had an affair with Nick Davis, a

revelation that led to the shocking news that Phil was actually Amy's son, not Ruth's. When it came out in the open, Amy did the noble thing; she made herself scarce from Pine Valley. (This exit fulfilled the original terms of actress Rosemary Prinz's agreement with Agnes Nixon. Looking for an ace in the hole to start *All My Children* off, Agnes had approached the very popular actress to see if she would return to soaps, which she had publicly denounced years earlier. The two soap veterans struck up a deal: Rosemary would do a six-month stint to get *All My Children* off the ground if Agnes would agree to let her play the part of an activist, speaking out against such things as the Vietnam War.)

With Amy gone, Lincoln Tyler was on the market for a wife again. And once again he chose a woman who did not meet his mother's approval. Kitty Shea had also been involved with Nick Davis, in fact she had been married to him. She had a questionable background and was an unstable type. Phoebe concocted a rather wild scheme to drive the couple apart. She hired a woman to act as Kitty's long-lost mother and lure her away from Pine Valley. After many

Karen Gorney, *who played Tara for many years,* left All My Children *and won a prize film role—co-starring with John Travolta in* Saturday Night Fever.

Larry Fleischman (Benny Sago).

Susan Lucci (Erica Kane).

complications, including the mock death of the "mother," complete with funeral, the truth came out and the plan backfired. Not only did Linc and Kitty get back together, the "mother" was taken in as part of the family and lived with them until Kitty died.

Phoebe also worked hard to prevent the marriage of Chuck, her grandson, and Donna, an ex-prostitute, at one point going so far as to enlist the aid of Donna's former pimp. She's also resorted to blackmail, thievery, and feigned paralysis to prevent her husband from divorcing her to marry Mona Kane.

And that is *All My Children,* or as writer Dan Wakefield titled his book on the show, *All Her Children*—the families, characters, and town under the watchful eye of Agnes Nixon. There are the two main families, the Tylers and the Martins, four generations apiece. There are their friends and neighbors as well. And all seem determined to make Pine Valley a peaceful place to come home to no matter what.

(L to r) Hugh Franklin (Dr. Charles Tyler) *and Susan Lucci* (Erica Kane) *leaving the studio at the end of the workday.*

A Fan Remembers

Martha N. lives in Boston. She's 33 years old and has two children. She says:

"When I sat down to watch All My Children *today, I realized I'd been following the program since the very first episode. I can't think of anything else in my life that's been so constant.*

"I got hooked on the show because I was home for the first time in my life with a one-year-old daughter who had a lung infection. I began sleeping my afternoons away with her, feeling more and more depressed that I was losing the only time left for myself during the day. I decided I needed a new ritual for her naptime. I read about the premiere of All My Children, *and relevant drama sounded more sophisticated to me than soap opera. It wasn't, but it got me hooked.*

"I guess I'm what you'd call a closet fan. At least I was for a long time. Things have changed now about people's attitudes toward watching soap operas, but back then I never told anybody I watched. The image of watching daytime TV was too tied up in other things I felt ambivalent about—being a housewife, staying at home. I would rush to turn off the TV if the phone or doorbell rang. I would lie rather than admit I watched a soap opera.

"When I had been following All My Children *for about a year, I spent a week with my sister and got her hooked on the show too. Then she moved near me to take a job, and we'd keep each other up on the story when either of us missed it. One day I called her and left a message with her husband that Phil was missing in action in Vietnam and Tara was pregnant with his child and Chuck wanted to marry her to be the baby's father. Carl assumed I was talking about some real-life people. He called my sister immediately.*

"I guess the truth is that I can't be very objective about why I watch All My Children. *I think a lot of the acting is really good, but that's what makes it tolerable, that's not what makes me watch it. I get impatient with the fact that the drama is all based on deception—on people not being straightforward with one another. But maybe that's not so unlike life. I also get upset with the sex role stereotyping. I wish the show had just one gutsy woman who wasn't also bitchy—and who wouldn't sell her grandfather for a man. I could keep picking the program apart without answering why I watch it. I'm not sure. It's just that it feels like* my *soap opera—a tale spun out for my entertainment. I've watched since the beginning. It's part of my life.*

"Up until the early fifties, people tended to be born, raised, and die within a fifty-mile radius. Families were routinely three and four generations. These days everybody you know has children or parents living three thousand miles away. There is less continuity in people's lives than there once was. What draws people to soap operas is the chance to regain that feeling of continuity."—Byrna Laub, editor/founder, Daytime Serial Newsletter

Fan Magazines

Soap opera fans are well cared for with about sixteen different magazines that keep tabs on the world of soaps. They keep fans up to date on the private lives of actors and actresses—who married whom, who's getting divorced, whose marriage was just barely saved. There are feature articles about the making of soaps and soap opera history. Some magazines include editorials and others keep track of the storylines of the shows. Since for many years the conventional media was determined to ignore or ridicule soaps, this proliferation of fan magazines was the one way the soap opera world could look after itself.

The soap opera magazine business has its ups and downs, but generally business is good, with an average circulation of about 340,000 and a total readership of perhaps twice that. There are also a number of nationally syndicated newspaper columns and small newsletters that feature plot summaries and late-breaking events.

The fan magazines can be innovative. For example, when he was editor of Afternoon TV, Milburn Smith initiated the first awards for daytime TV, awards that predated the daytime Emmys. Afternoon TV holds secret balloting among its staff and announces winners at an annual New York banquet.

Paul Denis was the first to get into the soap opera fan magazine business, starting Daytime TV some twelve years ago. As TV editor of the New York Post, Denis was aware of a burgeoning soap opera audience. Before starting his own magazine Denis and his wife did a soap column for TV Picture Life. It ran under his wife's name because the publisher felt that a column on soaps had to have a woman's by-line. Nowadays Denis supervises publication of one monthly, a bimonthly, and several annuals, Who's Who in Daytime TV and TV's Greatest Daytime Stories among them.

"When we got into the field nobody was covering daytime, and the response was so terrific that we just kept putting out more and more," Denis explains. "Fans were hungry for information about soap people because they saw them every day in their own homes and got to like them. There's a tremendous emotional impact when you see someone in your home every day."

Paul Denis's office in downtown Manhattan has become an informal drop-in center for the soap opera world. Denis encourages actors and producers to visit at any time. He also operates an informal information center, with research files that span an entire ten-foot wall in his office. Denis's phone rings all through the day with requests for information. Stars call him to chat. He knows about their families, their lives, their career problems, their plans.

On the other coast is Bryna Laub, who in a different way has also turned her position as editor of a soap opera magazine into an advocacy program for the world of soaps. She is editor/founder of Daytime Serial Newsletter, a monthly magazine that specializes in covering the plotlines of the shows.

"When I was in grade school, I used to listen to the radio soaps," she recalls. "In college I watched soap operas in the student union, and when I graduated and taught school there was a TV in my classroom, and I'd watch the shows while I graded papers."

When she had her first baby, she decided to quit teaching. Because women's liberation was the topic of the day many of her working friends would call up to warn her against turning into a hausfrau. "They'd give me a sermon, and then after the sermon the next question would be, 'Did you see my show? What happened on my show today?'" After some months of keeping her friends up to date on soap stories, Bryna Laub's husband joked, "You could probably get paid to stay home and watch those shows."

Four years later, by one report, she was grossing over a quarter of a million dollars a year. Her "newsletter" with its in-depth plotlines of soap opera stories, serves 85,000 readers. Students who can't cut classes to watch soaps, women who have gone back to work, families who have been stationed overseas, all subscribe to the magazine.

The Laub home now has seven TV sets—three in the living room and one each in the bedroom, the dining room, and the office. Sophisticated video equipment records the stories and a staff of ten watch the shows and write plot summaries.

"Iris appears at Mac's townhouse," reads one month's review of Another World, "and makes nasty insinuations about Pat's being with him while Rachel's at home with Ken. Mac walks out. Iris continues with Pat, but Pat leaves too. Iris manipulates herself in to see Keith Morrison, an old friend, whom Iris wants to take over her legal affairs. Keith doesn't want any more clients. . . ."

Bryna Laub has made the soaps her own cause célèbre and appears on talk shows from coast to coast to dispel the negative stigma attached to soap opera. She is also a walking encyclopedia when it comes to soap stories and soap characters. As a regular guest on AM San Francisco, she answers questions from fans, sometimes interjecting her own analysis. "Dee's a pocket neurotic," she explained to one caller. "She's the kind of person that no matter how much someone tries to show that they love her, she just won't believe it."

Paul Denis of Daytime TV, Milburn Smith of Afternoon TV, and Bryna Laub of Daytime Serial Newsletter, each in his own way, have made a contribution to the soap world. Denis gave it a home, Smith gave it awards, and Laub gave it a voice. Many soap actors don't like the gossipy stories on their personal lives that the magazines generally feature, but they all acknowledge that the magazines help with their careers.

Soaps Go to College

In addition to the college craze of watching soap operas in student unions during lunchtime, soaps have developed a following among academics who have begun to apply the same systematic study to them that they have done to other aspects of American life. The Modern Language Association, an association of college English teachers, presented a session on soap opera at one of their annual gatherings in New York:

497. Special Session: Ideology and Narrative Technique in Television: A Semiological Analysis of Gynocentric Serial Dramas (4:00-5:15 P.M., Morgan A. Hilton) Discussion Leaders. English Showalter, Jr., Rutgers Univ., and Joan DeJean, Univ. of Pennsylvania.
Papers to be Discussed.
1. ''The Languages of Mary Hartman.'' Gerald Prince, Univ. of Pennsylvania.
2. ''Soap Time.'' Dennis Porter, Univ. of Massachusetts, Amherst.
3. ''Queen for a Day at a Time.'' Kate Ellis, Rutgers Univ., Livingston Coll.
Discussants: Carol Murphy, Mount Holyoke Coll.; Ronald Rosebottom, Ohio State Univ.

Ms. Margot Norris is a college teacher who has devoted some study to soap operas. While working in the English Department of the University of Tulsa in Oklahoma she offered a course entitled "The Genres of Television Drama," and soaps were among the topics of discussion. Below are some of Ms. Norris's thoughts as a result of her research into the field.

I find soap operas fascinating because they seem to utilize the potential of television as a unique medium better than any other television genre. Television is essentially a dramatic medium. But unlike either live drama or commercial film, it has a potential daily audience. Because they are serial in form, soap operas use the continuity of daily television to create long and complicated narratives, like those found in eighteenth- and nineteenth-century novels. Soap operas are therefore unique because they fuse two literary genres, the drama and the novel; this fusion is made possible precisely by the nature of television.

I am convinced that the appeal of soap opera is not its content, but its form. In other words, what keeps women (and men, it seems) riveted to their favorite shows is probably less their sympathy with the sad plight of the characters than the carefully controlled suspense and irony which result from combining the intricate, novelistic plot with the dramatic revelation. For example, illegitimate pregnancies and illicit affairs are less interesting as sociological facts than because they provide instant secrets which promise a dramatic revelation. The affair between Barbara Weaver and John Randolph of Another World a few years ago was utterly banal in its content and circumstance: an affair between a lawyer

and his colleague during late evenings at work. But we watched hypnotically as Pat Randolph slowly and painfully pieced together various clues that would lead to her eventual discovery of the secret. Meanwhile the brilliant Barbara actively conspired to throw dozens of red herrings in Pat's path, using her bachelor colleague, Mark Venable, as a screen to make Pat pair Barbara and Mark, rather than Barbara and John, in her mind, and finally making Pat suspect her best friend Lenore Curtin as the "other woman." This complicated situation generated wonderful moments of irony on the show. Pat, for example, would gush to her husband about how Barbara and Mark looked like two lovebirds, while her husband, John, writhed with jealousy. This is precisely the reason why casual soap opera watchers fail to realize the fascination of the programs. A casual watcher turning on the set one day and seeing Pat and Barbara in cozy conversation would assume they are merely two women friends exchanging confidences. Only a program veteran would recognize that one woman is manipulating the other, pumping her for information, leading her to erroneous conclusions. The individual half-hour or hour segments often seem vapid in content to a new viewer, at the same time that they are laden with irony and significance for someone familiar with a show's ten-year history. For example, a casual encounter between Rachel and Russ Matthews takes on special significance to the viewer aware that they were once married and that during this marriage Rachel conceived a child by another man. One of the truly great moments of soap opera irony occurred a few years ago on Return to Peyton Place during Mike Rossi's wedding. While Stephen sang the theme from Zefferelli's Romeo and Juliet—a song all about "love denied"—the camera slowly panned from one character to another, from the bridegroom himself, who loved Connie Carson, not the bride, to Alison, who loved Rodney Harrington, from Rodney, who loved his wife, Betty, to Betty, who loved her first husband, Stephen, and so on—an abundance of "love denied" all around.

One of the great misconceptions about soap operas is that they are characterized by many emotional and hysterical scenes. Quite the opposite is the case. Most soap opera plots are propelled by repression, by the reluctance of characters to gossip, to tell each other secrets, to interfere with each other's business, and to confront each other in a way that would cause a scene. "Near encounters"—someone almost hearing or telling a secret or almost witnessing an incriminating scene, provide much of the suspense on the shows. For example, Alice Frame's failure to confront her husband, Steve, and Rachel when she overhears their conversation leads to further complications, including Steve and Rachel's marriage and Rachel's temporary triumph. The conversation (about Rachel and Steve being together the night of Alice's miscarriage) is skillfully engineered by Rachel. Rachel must address the conversation to two listeners at once—to Steve, next to her, in such a way that he will not suspect an ulterior motive, and simultaneously to the eavesdropping Alice. Scenes like this could have been lifted out of an eighteenth-century nōvel; they are particularly effective because instead of reading them, we see them enacted dramatically.

Much of the content of TV soap operas is determined by the form. For example, the soaps have traditionally featured the "crisis" professions—doctors, lawyers, newspaper people—because of their dramatic potential. Traditionally, many soap operas have a business at its center (Peyton Industries, Frame Enterprises, Delaney Brands) in order to complicate the domestic plots with issues of money and power. For example, the identity of the father of Betty Harrington's child in Return to Peyton Place was of great importance because if the child were Rodney's it would rightfully inherit the Peyton fortune, whereas if it were Stephen's (it was) it would wrongfully inherit. Mary Hartman, Mary Hartman broke new ground in this respect by focusing on the assembly workers rather than the executives of the central Fernwood industry. Instead of corporate corruption and rivalries, union corruption and rivalries form a dramatic issue. The form of the soap opera also requires illicit activity on all fronts, domestic, professional, and criminal. Only when there is illicit activity are there secrets, and only when there are secrets can there be suspense and revelation. The short-lived soap opera How to Survive a Marriage failed precisely because it tried to depict a modern society so liberated that there were few taboos. Everything was aboveboard, no secrets, no suspense, and the show folded quickly. The soap operas must keep alive the fantasy of a repressed Victorian society for their own survival.

"I think that if for nothing else I will always love daytime television soap operas for being the only medium that sent me a different message during that dreary post-divorce holiday season. On Christmas Eve that year I watched one soap opera after another and was relieved to find that the lives of the perfectly nice people portrayed were not all rosy with fa-la-la-de-da, but ones with troubles, confusions, and traumas, and whose pain and intensity were heightened by the pressure of the holidays."

—Dan Wakefield writing in All Her Children

the Young and the Restless

WHEN IS A SOAP OPERA also a paperback novel, an A.M. radio hit single, and a record album featuring such greats as "The Genoa City Theme," "Blue Images," and "Love is Gone"? What soap has its name inscribed on blue windbreakers for all members of the cast? *The Young and the Restless* is soap opera cult, but not in the campy manner of the devotion to *Dark Shadows*, the now-defunct returned-from-the-dead spooky soap. *The Young and the Restless* is mainline soap, and its cult following is a result of the fact that it's younger, sexier, and more glamorous than anything that's come before.

The show premiered in 1973, and within three short years on the air it had defied the most time-honored of soap opera canons—that it takes years of careful wooing to build up an audience. It moved right to the top of the Nielsen ratings, won five different Emmys in its first two years of production, and was relentlessly voted the top soap opera in magazine popularity polls.

What's the recipe for instant success in the lucrative soap opera world? For one thing, it takes beauty. The producers of *The Young and the Restless* gathered a cast together that sometimes more closely resembles a beauty contest than a dramatic production. In addition, it has the youngest cast ever assembled for a soap. Most of the actors—tanned, healthy looking, trying to break into nighttime TV and movies—are in their twenties; few had ever done soaps before.

These were conscious casting decisions. The producers wanted to stay away from familiar soap faces,

---

"We spend more time with each other than we do with our own families. We get to know each other pretty well." —JOHN CONBOY, *executive producer*

disassociating this new soap from the dreariness of soaps past and giving it an upbeat, modern image.

"We like to have good production values," explains producer Patricia Wenig. "That means beautiful sets, interesting sets, lighting that's well done, not just flat. And it also means we like to have good-looking people doing the parts. As John Conboy, executive producer, once said, and I agree with him, we're going to be with these people five days a week, so why shouldn't they be attractive to look at?

The Foster family comes from the other side of the tracks in Genoa City. They're poor and Liz Foster worked first in a factory, then as a maid to support her family and help her two sons along with their careers. Here, Snapper Foster (originally played by William Gray Espy) *and Liz Foster* (Julianna McCarthy).

You'd rather look at a pretty face five days a week than an ugly, unattractive one."

The Young and the Restless does have the best production values—lighting, sets, costumes, etc.—of any show on daytime television, but sometimes it's so perfect and glossy, it seems almost like a parody of the look it's trying to achieve.

The strongest feature of *The Young and the Restless* is its storyline, which was created and written by William Bell, recognized by his colleagues as "the best storyteller in the business." Bell began with Irna Phillips in 1956 on *The Guiding Light*. From there he went with her to *As the World Turns*, which he wrote for nine years. Then, when *Days of Our Lives* came on the air in 1965 and had difficulty gaining an audience, Bell was brought on to write the show. It became such a success that he was asked by all three networks, and Proctor & Gamble Productions as well, to create a show of his own, and he negotiated the deal for *The Young and the Restless* even before he knew what it would be about. For several years he planned the storyline for *Days* and did both the story and the scripts for *The Young and the Restless*, an undertaking that required, by his own account, sixteen hours a day for six to seven days a week.

"I knew I wanted a rivalry between two sisters," Bell wrote of his early conception of *The Young and the Restless*. "I knew I wanted one of the sisters to be shy and introverted, the other very confident and caught up in today's world with a great drive toward success and recognition. Leslie's background in music and Lorie's talent toward writing evolved from that. Both young women, I felt, would be richly identifiable. As would be a younger sister in love with love, the romanticist, Chris. And finally, every girl's baby sister, Peggy.

"I knew too that I wanted a poor family in the overall plan with two brothers I hoped might be an inspiration to other young men—self-educated, family-oriented, both about to embark on careers in professions, who succeeded because they had the attitude that 'for things to happen, you've got to

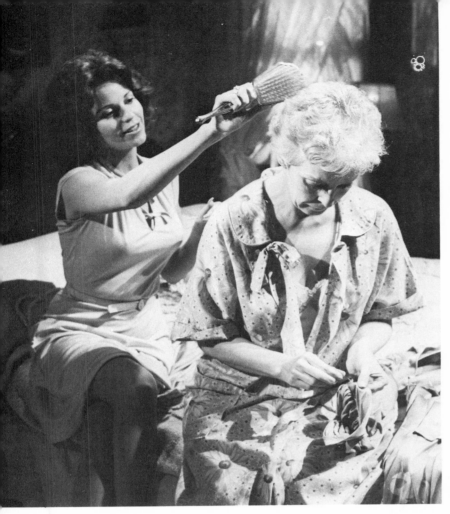

Jill Foster (Brenda Dixon) *with her mother.*

The Foster brothers—Snapper and Greg (originally played by Jim Houghton), *a doctor and a lawyer respectively.*

Jennifer Brooks (Dorothy Green) *and Stuart Brooks* (Robert Colbert). *"I never believed people could talk as much in real life as they do on soaps until recently when I visited a small town for a few days with my daughter, and there I was right in the middle of a soap opera. In a small town people don't have the theater and museums and cultural things to talk about so that life literally revolves around their families and sitting and talking about their problems. Suddenly I had my eyes opened. Life does move along like soap opera in small towns. I think I just never stood still with the same group of people long enough to find this out."* —DOROTHY GREEN

make them happen!' I planned to have a younger sister who worked so her brothers could make it through college. The Fosters—Snapper, Greg, Jill, and their hard-working mother, Liz—would be a tight family unit.

"Also I wanted a mystery character of sorts. A man around thirty who appeared as the show began, a man escaping his past—in search of a future. Yet a man with credentials. This character, of course, became Brad Elliot.

"In other words, I knew I wanted a broad base of young people—wholesome, identifiable, appealing —in situations and stories that reflected a segment of contemporary life."

Zoom in on Genoa City, where Stuart Brooks, publisher of the city newspaper, and his stylish wife, Jennifer, have a family of four grown daughters. No two are alike, yet they are all beauties. None is likely to be content as just a wife and mother, yet each, in her own way, puts the love of a man above all else.

When Brad Elliot showed up in Genoa City ready to assume his new identity, he met Stuart Brooks, who took an immediate liking to him and gave him a job on the newspaper. In his former life Brad had

(L to r) Chris, Peggy, and Jennifer Brooks—a mother with two of her four daughters. "When we first started the show I mimicked some of Dorothy's hand gestures and facial expressions because when you're living in a family you do pick up things like that from each other. My own mother watching the show saw that and said, 'It's as if you're really her own daughter.' " —TRISH STEWARD (Chris)

Sisters (l to r) Peggy Brooks (Pamela Solow) and Chris Brooks Foster (Trish Stewart). "Acting on a soap with an ongoing character is an odd combination of Gestalt therapy and pyschodrama. In a funny way, by playing certain personality traits out on screen, I found it harder to continue to do them in my own life. For example, I have always been the type with a social worker complex, and my character has that too. She's always there for people, she always knows their problems, she always tries to help them out. Through acting out some of these stories I began to see that you really have to start at home and help yourself first. Sometimes it just doesn't help to take responsibility away from another person. Doing the show and playing my character has helped me grow as a person and learn new things about myself." —TRISH STEWART

Janice Lynde, the actress who originated the role of Leslie Brooks, a talented concert pianist, is actually also a pianist herself. When she played piano in a scene, it was her playing, not a recorded sound track.

Wealthy international playboy Lance Prentiss (John McCook) encouraged Leslie in her career as a pianist. He later married the fourth Brooks sister, Lorie.

Snapper got involved with Sally McGuire (Lee Crawford), a waitress at Pierre's, the local nightclub. He got her pregnant, then returned to Chris. When Sally found out that Snapper and Chris were married, she tried to kill herself, then left town with the baby.

Meanwhile, Chris, another sister, fell in love with Snapper, a medical student from the poor Foster family. Stuart Brooks didn't approve of his daughter's choice of a boyfriend, but when he tried to break them up Chris got angry and moved out of the house to try to make it on her own. She ended up getting raped by a man she met in a bar who insisted on walking her home. For months, both the Fosters and the Brookses were embroiled in the trauma of Chris's efforts to get justice against her attacker.

As for the youngest Brooks daughter, Peggy, she was busy falling in love with one of her teachers at college, who was married, although she didn't know it. Then Peggy ended up the victim of *The Young and the Restless*'s second rape. Traumatized, she hid in her room, wouldn't face anyone, and was only

been a psychiatrist/neurosurgeon living in Chicago. When he operated on his fiancee's son (whom he discovered was his own son) and the boy died, Brad ran away to begin a new life. Through his new boss, Brad met daughter Leslie.

Leslie had devoted herself so long to her piano studies that she was awkward and shy around men. When Brad finally won her confidence, Leslie's competitive sister Lorie returned from Paris and tried to steal him away. This caused Leslie to have a nervous breakdown. With Brad's help, she recovered, and they were married. Later, their marriage was shattered when Brad started to go blind and decided to run away rather than tell his wife. When he returned, it was too late. They were divorced and Brad left town.

The romance of Chris Brooks and Snapper Foster: Chris and Snapper fell in love, but Snapper wasn't sure he was ready for marriage, and Chris's father, Stuart Brooks, disapproved of the match anyway since he wanted his daughter to marry someone of a higher social standing.

slowly induced to come out and identify her attacker in court, who got off on a technicality. The attack left her emotionally disturbed and fearful of sex.

In recent years, the rivalry between Lorie and Leslie has continued. Lorie met and married Lance Prentiss, a wealthy business tycoon who had been instrumental in encouraging Leslie in her concert career and who secretly had deep feelings for her. Under a pseudonym, Lorie had also written a novel detailing Leslie's breakdown, among other embarrassing revelations. When the book became a bestseller, there was speculation about the authorship, and Leslie was once again plunged into depression thanks to her sister. Lance, as usual, came to the rescue, they spent one night together, and she ended up pregnant. Not long afterward, Lorie came upon them as Lance was comforting Leslie with a not-very-platonic kiss. Both to further her own ambitions and get back at Leslie, who she wrongly assumed was trying to break up her marriage, Lorie decided to publicly acknowledge authorship of the controversial novel.

There is speculation by some local observers that the Genoa City of *The Young and the Restless* is based loosely on a real-life town located ten miles from Lake Geneva, Minnesota, where writer William Bell spends his summers. Whether this is the case or not, what is true is that Bell has tied his stories into many very real and contemporary subjects, which he prefers to think of as ''informing'' viewers rather than ''educating'' them.

''I believe television writing is more than an opportunity,'' explains Bell. ''It's a great responsibility. We writers have the power to influence millions

Snapper Foster and Chris Brooks's long-awaited wedding.

of lives daily.'' He has introduced problems of particular concern to women—rape, overeating, alcoholism, breast cancer. He has also incorporated the dangers of smoking into everyday life in Genoa City; Snapper Foster plucks cigarettes out of people's mouths and delivers a stern lecture every time he catches someone smoking.

The Young and the Restless is meant to appeal especially to young people. It has more explicit talk of sex than any serial before, and possibly more seduction scenes, bedroom scenes, and dresses unzipped slowly down the spine than anywhere else on television. Everything on screen is more modern, more fashionable; in some ways, that old term ''soap opera'' no longer seems to hold.

Yet underneath this compelling contemporary gloss, all the old soap opera formulas are still in force as much as ever. Scratch a William Bell and you find an Irna Phillips. Scratch *The Young and the Restless* and there's *As the World Turns*. Now we have four sisters instead of the standard two brothers, and that allows the more modern stories that portray women as individuals in their own right. We have wealthier characters and a new cosmopolitan style of life. And we have middle-class professionals who have branched out from the tradition of doctors and lawyers to include writers, newspaper publishers, legal aide workers, and artistic types. But the soap core of a stable central family is still there. And then there are the old themes—threats to family solidarity deriving from jealousy among siblings, clashes of economic class, and ever-enticing tales of adultery—remain.

It's now nearly half a century since Irna Phillips had her character Mother Moynihan explain, '' . . . I'm thinking that a country is only as strong as its weakest home. When you're after destroyin' those things which make up a home, you're destroyin' people. . . .'' And still the likes of William Bell are carrying on that tradition. Bell's faith in the family goes right down to the wire; he named the young folks in Genoa City after his own children. He has a Billy (Snapper's real name), a Bradley, and a Lauralee (Lorie's full name). Despite the new glamour and sex in *The Young and the Restless*, it still drives the main point home—the thing to defend in order to be happy in America is the loyalty and sanctity of home.

Mother and son: Brock Reynolds (Beau Kayzer) *and Kay Chancellor* (Jeanne Cooper). *Brock believes in the healing powers of religious faith. His mother, a wealthy and troublemaking widow, battles with loneliness and alcoholism.*

Peggy Brooks (Pamela Solow), *the youngest Brooks daughter, didn't realize the man she was falling in love with, Jack Curtis, one of her teachers at college, was already a married man. Jack was growing tired of his marriage, though, and of his wife, who was getting more and more overweight and had ceased growing as a person.*

Joanne Curtis (Kay Heberle) *became very overweight due to both sorrow over a miscarriage and the neglect of her husband, Jack* (Anthony Herrera). *Viewers watched as she lost weight gradually on the show and finally pulled herself and her life together again.*

Casting the Soaps

David Hasselhoff replaced William Gray Espy in the role of Snapper.

The primary rule of soap opera is that audience identification with characters makes for high ratings. That's why, next to writing the stories, casting the right actors is considered the most important part of the business. Fans' loyalty to characters makes a show endure. If a producer can come up with the right actor with the right personality to project into the part, viewers will tune in tomorrow after tomorrow.

John Conboy, executive producer of The Young and the Restless, a show as carefully cast as any, explains why casting is crucial. "We're not doing Shakespeare here or Ibsen where we'd be casting people to do a defined role that's been completely drawn by the author. Here we have to pay attention to the whole person, to the personality and personal charisma, because that's what's going to make the part. The personality has to come through on the screen, and if an actor doesn't have any personal charisma to begin with, you're sure not going to get it out of him when what you're doing in a soap is basically asking him to relax and play himself. We're looking for a personality that will come through on camera."

Harding Lemay, headwriter for Another World, wants actors who "will give me something to work from. When I see them on screen I want to see where they're leading me, and then I write for that quality, build on it to let it come out."

To replace Bill Epsy in the part of Snapper Foster in The Young and the Restless, John Conboy and producer Pat Wenig saw 175 people. Each actor read scenes with the various characters Snapper would be encountering on a regular basis. The chemistry—a term used to denote a special quality of interaction between two actors when they get into their parts—would have to be right with Snapper's wife, his mother, his sister, his father-in-law. "We had them read to see their ability as actors," Conboy explains, "but really, you can't tell that much until you get them on their feet in rehearsals and in front of the camera. More than acting we're looking for something that happens to us when an actor comes through the door." When David Hasselhoff walked into the office to test for the part, both Pat Wenig and John Conboy knew right away that he was the one they had been looking for. "He was the last person we saw. It often works out that way. We read and we read and we read and all of a sudden somebody walks through that door and explodes at us. And it's really intangible. It's something you just have to feel."

The time and money that went into casting Snapper isn't unusual. The Guiding Light's producer and casting director saw over 286 possible new Leslie Bauers before they chose Barbara Rodell some years ago.

In both these cases, since they were casting to replace an actor, not to introduce a new character to the show, the producers faced the problem of having to "cast up." To compensate for the loss of an actor the audience had grown to care about, producers feel they must give viewers something more than what they had—someone even better, more glamorous, more attractive, more sympathetic, or more volatile.

By the same token, producers usually feel a responsibility not to jolt viewers in recasting a part. Often they introduce a new actor in an ingenious or complicated way to cover for the change. When James Storm, who played Dr. Larry Wolek on One Life to Live, was to be replaced by a new actor, the writers concocted a storyline to facilitate the change. They had the character fall into a flaming storage closet, and when he emerged with third-degree burns, he was rushed to the hospital for an operation. The next time he was seen his face was wrapped in bandages and he was recovering from extensive plastic surgery. When the bandages were finally removed, a new face emerged—that of another actor, Michael Storm, the original actor's brother.

Casting soap opera is like giving birth to walking, talking adults. Often it involves adding another member to an existing family. He has to fit in, it has to make sense, and most important of all, both the writer and the viewers have got to grow to like him.

Some Soapy Subjects: Breast Cancer and Rape

Dorothy Green and Trish Stewart played mother and daughter. As Chris Brooks, Trish portrayed the victim of a rape. Dorothy Green, who played Jennifer until the character died of a heart condition, fought a screen battle with breast cancer. In both storylines viewers were taken through a documentarylike exploration of the subject. Chris got help from the local "rape crisis center"; Jennifer Brooks had the help of "Reach for Recovery," a real-life organization. After these storylines were aired, Reach for Recovery and rape crisis centers across the country reported increases in requests for help.

Dorothy Green on the Breast Cancer Story

Cancer is a subject that is not foreign to me at all. My late husband died of cancer, and two of his sisters had breast cancer. One died because she hid her head in the sand and refused to admit there was a problem until it was too late. The other had a mastectomy and is still alive today.

When they told me I was going to do a cancer story, I was less than thrilled. I knew it was going to be difficult. Then in the midst of doing the whole thing my mother died suddenly. I was just about to go off to surgery in the story and there was no way they could write me out, so I was back at work right away going through all the business of a major operation.

"It's a great ego leveler to have your identity totally involved with a character. I'm Jennifer Brooks, that's it. I went up to Las Vegas during the time in the story when I was having the affair with Bruce. It was absolutely eye-opening for me not to be able to get through the lobby of Caesar's Palace without half a dozen people grabbing my arm, both men and women, and saying, 'Jen—are you going to go back to Stuart? Are you going to stay with Bruce?' " —DOROTHY GREEN

It helped me to go through this difficult period in my life by knowing that this was a storyline that could help someone. If even one woman's life was saved through what we were doing, then it was definitely worth it to me. We had lots of women write in afterward to say that as a result of the story they went for breast checkups and Pap smears. Some wrote that they caught a problem in time.

A close friend of mine who worked with the Reach for Recovery program and had gone through a mastectomy herself, came to the set to make sure I was doing things accurately. Getting her opinions on things was very interesting. For example, she said that from her experience working with breast cancer patients, it's pretty much the kind of person you are before the whole thing happens that determines how you're going to handle it. I myself have always been a positive sort of person, and that's how I always played Jennifer Brooks. But in this breast cancer story they kept writing scripts with the most negative things for me to say, as if Jennifer had suddenly taken on an attitude of just giving up. Viewers had already started writing to me about it. One woman said, "I'm trying to deal with this situation too. I'm not half as good-looking as Jennifer is. I don't have a husband and a family to fall back on that loves me. If Jennifer isn't coping with it, how do you expect me to?" Finally I went to them and said I thought it would be doing the women of America a great disservice if Jennifer continued to be so negative about this. After that, they began to change the scripts.

Later on we put together a mini-documentary about the breast cancer story, taking taped portions of the story all the way from when she first discovered she had breast cancer right through the operation. We showed it at the American Film Institute in Los Angeles during a weekend they had for women, and I was there to answer questions. One woman followed me outside in order to continue to talk to me privately, and she told me she had watched the story while she was in the hospital recovering from her own mastectomy. She explained that at first it had been just too painful for her to watch it on TV, but then little by little she began following it regularly, and she said it helped her through her own recovery.

"Once I did the Johnny Carson show and somebody came up to me and said, 'Are you somebody?' And I said, 'Well, it depends, I mean, aren't you?' He said, 'I mean are you one of those actresses? Do you do stuff?' Then he made me wait while he brought over his friends and said, 'I've got one.' " —TRISH STEWART (Chris-Brooks Foster)

Trish Stewart on the Rape Story

The rape story also helped viewers with information. We got lots of mail about it, just as we did for the cancer story. The story showed viewers some of the problems that rape victims face, and it brought in the existence of "rape crisis centers" that women can go to for help. In the storyline Chris didn't want to go to trial. She didn't want to go to the lineup. She just wanted to forget it, which is the attitude most women have in that situation. But then in the story a woman came from the rape crisis center and helped her to see the things she could do, how to get counseling and help.

After that first rape story I got a lot of mail saying that I asked for it because I had put myself into a position where I could get raped. I think one of the reasons for doing the second rape story in the plotline was so there would be no way anybody could make the accusation that there was provocation on the part of the victim. Peggy was raped by someone she didn't even know, someone she had never met. This time there could be no doubt. There was no way to blame the woman.

We did one episode of the show in which we tried to give a lot of information about rape so that women watching would know how to protect themselves. Basically it was me sitting at a table and going over the dailies of an article I had written on rape for my father's newspaper. A man sitting opposite asked me what I was doing and I explained. So we sat there reading the article through together and talking about the different points it raised. It was a way of injecting more useful information into the storyline. It was a bit awkward to try to make it sound conversational, but I believe it was something important to do in the show.

Brad Elliot Arrives in Genoa City

When The Young and the Restless *first came on the air, it started with the story of Brad Elliot, a young man who ran away from Chicago and a former life there as a doctor to take on a new identity and begin life over. As a doctor he had been involved in an operation on the son of his fiancée (who he found out was his own son too), and when the boy died, he couldn't face staying. On his way out of Chicago, he was held up at gun point, lost his wallet, and ended up beaten unconscious. He hitched a ride with a truck driver who brought him to Genoa City. When he went to eat at Pierre's Restaurant and discovered he didn't have enough money to pay the bill, Stuart Brooks, publisher of Genoa City's newspaper, came to his rescue and paid. Later the two men got talking and Stu offered Brad a job on the paper. When Brad met Stuart Brook's daughter, Leslie, a very shy and very talented concert pianist, the two fell in love and eventually married.*

The Dragon Who Turned into a Prince by Tom Hallick

Tom Hallick played Brad Elliot, the man who arrived in Genoa City determined to leave his troublesome past behind him. But he accumulated a new troublesome past, and when his marriage to Leslie broke up for good, he left Genoa City again.

Before Tom Hallick left his role and the show, he talked about how he got to The Young and the Restless *and what he's gotten out of it.*

Prior to The Young and the Restless, *or* "Y & R," *as it's affectionately called, I had a rather forgettable role in a series called* Search, *which has since gone on to that great film library in the sky. But the very week the show was canceled, I got a call from my agent telling me that they'd been looking for someone for a part in a serial for three months and still hadn't found the right person. I'd never done a serial before, and even though it was good money, I wasn't that anxious to do one. But I went in anyway to test for the role of Brad. I think they'd seen over a hundred different people by the time they got around to me, but I guess I was what they had been looking for. I decided, why not, it couldn't really hurt to do it for a couple of years.*

In certain ways I was more prepared than most people in the cast for this kind of thing because I had done a lot of theater. My background was theater. I did my first play when I was six years old. I was the reluctant dragon. I'll never forget it. I sang a little song. I was the dragon who turned into a prince.

I happen to think that The Young and the Restless *is the best show on daytime television. It deals with problems that are of interest to young people. I get a lot of invitations from college students to come talk with them. And I get quite a lot of mail. Part of it is the usual: I love you, please send a picture and an autograph. People think they know you, and they write you as a friend. Some write to you as an imagined lover, as someone they hope someday to meet, or as someone they might be in love with. Most of the mail, though, is from people, like the college students, who write with specific knowledge of what it is to put out a television show, and they write to comment on the work itself or the development of the character. Videotape is like an X ray. You can't put anything over on people. You've got to produce.*

I love getting mail and I read all of it. I've gotten behind in answering, but I insist on writing back myself rather than hiring one of those services that sends out a mimeographed piece of something and a picture. The letters I answer first are the ones that come from foreign countries. [The Young and the Restless has been shown in Tokyo, Manila, Singapore, the Philippines, Australia, and Yugoslavia.] I answer mail from other countries first because I think of myself as a mini-ambassador, and I want to create a good impression of Americans.

If you act on a show like Y&R, people recognize you wherever you go. If I go into a department store, people go nuts. They come up to me to talk, ask questions, ask for autographs. Sometimes going out in public can be a bit overwhelming. I once went to a golf tournament in North Carolina and ended up being mobbed by the crowd. Hundreds of people surrounded me and literally tore the shirt off my back. They had ballpoint pens held out to get my autograph, and when I finally got free, there were pen marks all over my chest.

I suppose I've become a sex symbol of sorts. If that's what people think I am, fine, there's nothing wrong with that.

The Job of the Producer: Making Soap

The producer and headwriter are the VIPs of any soap. Together they have godlike power over the imaginary world of their own creation. By casting, planning storylines, and deciding the interpretation of character, they create life, undo it, and ultimately are only answerable to one higher authority—the Nielsen ratings. John Conboy, executive producer of The Young and the Restless, is considered one of the best in the soap business; producer Patricia Wenig works with him as a "right-hand woman." Together, they have an almost eerie dedication and seriousness of purpose. Standing in the control room with the script notebook opened between them, they review the day's scenes and wait for the rehearsal to begin.

Conboy, trim, casual, yet perfectly dressed, got his start in soaps in New York as a production assistant. He went from stage manager to associate director to actor, director, production supervisor, associate producer, and finally producer in a line of ascendency quite typical in the soap opera world.

They take their seats now in front of the TV monitors. Both are low-profile leaders, and their joint style is to expect rather than to command. Both are perfectionists, and as they settle in to watch the monitors now, it's as if they are daring the mechanical monsters to reveal even one flaw or error.

"We're looking for a lot of different things," Conboy explains. "We look to see that the shots are on the right people at the right time. And that doesn't necessarily mean on the people who are talking. We look at the composition of the shots, at the performance levels, at the lighting. We look to see if there are any objects in the frame that we don't want there. For example, if we're watching a scene, and we see that there's a lamp in the foreground, and we find ourselves concentrating more on the lamp than on what's going on in the scene, the lamp has got to come out of there. We listen to everything, the

dialogue, the music, and we keep track of the monitors to see that the shots that are coming up next are the ones we want to see there."

On screen, a shot is being prepared of wealthy Kay Chancellor about to snare a new husband. "Stop, we've got to change that. It's terrible," Conboy says. He strides out the door of the control room and onto the studio floor. Pat Wenig is just behind him. In a minute they're both back in their command chairs. "Okay, let's try it," Conboy orders, and when the scene is shot the director gets a nod of approval.

What does a soap opera producer do? "We do very little as long as everybody else is doing what they're supposed to be doing," Conboy answers. "We get very busy when the fabric we've created to produce the show falls apart. Our basic responsibility is putting together a unit of people and seeing that they do the best job they can. We're responsible for everyone who is involved in the production of the show, from stagehands to actors. A producer has to know the technical side of the business: how to run a studio, the machines, the videotape equipment, edit, put a crew together, and how to work with actors and union rules. We have to know how to work with writers, to know what goes into a script, how it's built, what can come out of it, what needs to be put into it. A producer has to be able to work with all different kinds of people, kind of a doctor-psychiatrist-father figure."

At the break between the run-through and the dress rehearsal, the actors meet in a circle of chairs on the studio floor. The director gently makes his criticisms.

Jaime Lyn Bauer (Lauralee Brooks Prentiss) rests her head against John Conboy's shoulder. As producers, Conboy and Wenig are the first to know of any personal problems that are going to get in the way of doing the show.

"It's very important to let people create," says Conboy. "And you can't create if you're oppressed or pushed down or scared. It's very important that both Pat and I keep our doors open to anybody who works with us."

Back in the control room, John bums a cigarette from Pat. The two smoke steadily now. "We work under a lot of pressure," he explains. "The hardest job anybody has to do in the television industry is a daytime serial. It's like putting out a new thirty-minute drama special every day of the week."

Part of a producer's job is keeping track of the audience reaction to his show. "I think everybody in this business pays attention to the Nielsen ratings," says Conboy. "People have nightmares about them. They affect everything that everybody in this business does. Creators, broadcasters, producers—we're all totally involved in the Nielsens."

There's also one person at The Young and the Restless office who has the job of reading through all the audience mail and making a monthly tabulation of its contents, giving a general picture of the various concerns of viewers and their reactions to storylines.

"The fan mail is sensational. We get a lot of mail from colleges, from professors as well as students. It's very gratifying to us. We get approximately 1500 letters a month from viewers. Half of that is to specific actors or actresses. The rest comes to the show. We pay a lot of attention to audience mail. I don't think we've ever changed a storyline because of audience mail, but people write in with a lot of good suggestions. For example, they'll write asking for more of a particular kind of story, like when we did the nun story we got letters from Sisters in convents all around the country. People were also very interested in the "overweight" story, and we got an enormous amount of mail suggesting diets for Joanne, asking what diet she was on, that sort of thing. We answer all the mail that comes in to the show."

After taping, the actors gather in a rehearsal hall upstairs to read through the next day's script. After the read-through, Conboy goes back over the script to make the cuts necessary to bring the episode down to the right length.

With the cuts made and announced, the actors move to the floor to begin rehearsing the next day's show with the director.

Conboy gathers up his cigarettes, his lighter, an empty coffee cup, the script, and starts heading back to his office, where's he's got a meeting scheduled for five o'clock.

"Why do I like producing?" He stops in the hall to take a moment to consider the question. "I like the pressure," he offers. "You have to like pressure. And you have to know how to deal with it. But I also like people not standing behind me and saying, 'I think you should do that.' I used to be a director and it used to drive me crazy when the producer would tell me what to do. I decided that in order not to deal with that I'd have to become a producer. I like shaping something that works. I like to be the one who stands behind people. And it's fun because we've got a hit. It's different if you've got a turkey. The worst job in the world for a producer is trying to make a turkey not a turkey." Conboy looks up and breaks into a very uncharacteristic grin. Though he doesn't say it, he's barnyards away from that.

"Program practices means that one of these little guys from upstairs comes down and sits in the booth and watches the run-through and he tells you if you're using a swear word that he doesn't want in. It gets crazy so we end up bargaining: 'I'll give you three damns for two hells,' or 'If you take only two damns today, you can have three hells tommorrow.' And they put a stopwatch on the credits to make sure they don't run over thirty seconds. They really have a terrible job, these guys. You're trying to get something to work dramatically and you have the line, 'Why the hell are you doing that?' The program practices guy sits there and says, 'Um, please cut that hell,' so you have the actor say, 'Why are you doing that?' and of course it's a completely different line." —JOHN CONBOY, *executice producer*

MARY HARTMAN
MARY HARTMAN

A WELL-MEANING AND languid housewife of Fernwood, Ohio, named Mary Hartman, has heard that her neighbor, high school coach Leroy Fedders, is feeling under the weather. She arrives at the doorstep bearing chicken soup. Leroy's wife, Blanche, has been trying to get Leroy to eat ("Starve a cold and feed a fever, or is it . . ."), but all Leroy is interested in is Seconal and a slug of bourbon. Mary knows better. "You mustn't take sleeping pills and liquor! You have to take some chicken soup!" And she sends Blanche off for a "really big bowl" to serve it in. "Now listen to me, Leroy Fedders . . . you're going to have a big bowl of chicken soup right now. They say it's terrific for anything that ails you. . . ."

The Fernwood ladies gather around the kitchen table: (l to r) Mary Hartman (Louise Lasser), *Loretta Haggers* (Mary Kay Place), *Cathy Shumway* (Debralee Scott), *and Martha Shumway* (Dody Goodman).

Leroy looks out through failing eyes. "Who's the 'they' that said that?"

Mary is certain of her sources. "An entire ethnic group. The Jewish people. They ought to know too. The Jewish people practically invented chicken soup, and an incredible amount of those people are doctors."

Blanche returns with a ladle and a soup bowl the size of a pig trough. "Here you go, Leroy," Mary says, "Now, I'm not going to give you a lot of vegetables because it's the soup part that goes right to the heart of a cold problem. The vegetables are good for building strong bodies, but you already have a strong body. It's the liquid soup that's going to gush through your system and kill those flu bugs wherever it finds them."

Mary sets the bowl down in front of Leroy, and she and Blanche depart. Blanche complains that Leroy's a terrible patient and Mary assures her, "Most men are. I think it's because they're not women. I mean,

The Mary Hartman, Mary Hartman *clan: (standing l to r)* Tom Hartman *(Greg Mullavey),* Heather Hartman *(Claudia Lamb),* Martha Shumway *(Dody Goodman),* Mary Hartman *(Louise Lasser),* Grandpa Larkin *(Victor Kilian), and (seated l to r)* George Shumway *(Philip Bruns), and* Cathy Shumway *(Debralee Scott).*

women have built-in pain—you know, cramps every month and labor when they have babies. Men just get burning sensations once in a while or heartburn—but that's really not pain."

As Mary and Blanche confer, the effects of Leroy's Seconal-bourbon binge begin to take hold. His head slowly sinks forward into the soup. He reaches his hand around to try to pull himself up by the back of his collar, but it's no use. Coach Leroy Fedders, one of Fernwood's meanest, died when he drowned in a bowl of chicken soup.

It was past midnight. I was listening on my end of the phone, but I was already half asleep. The person was talking about chicken soup, something about somebody dying in chicken soup. I was too tired to make it out. A few days later I overheard talk about death by soup again. It was a moment of déjà vu, but I couldn't place it. Then later, yet another person started chattering away about some guy who died in soup. "Well, what's all this about chicken soup?" I asked.

Patiently, if a little condescendingly, I was told about a new television show called *Mary Hartman, Mary Hartman,* a Norman Lear soap opera spoof. Within a week I was a Mary Hartman addict along with millions of others, many of whom were avowed television dropouts who had been wooed back to the tube by the word-of-mouth testimony that *Mary Hartman, Mary Hartman* was the best thing on TV since color.

Suddenly, everywhere—in elevators, during business phone calls, in restaurants—people who didn't even know each other were freely discussing the most intimate details of Fernwood, Ohio. "You think Mary will sleep with Foley?" "I think the gay neighbors are going to put the make on Tom." Infidelity, impotence, and homosexuality suddenly had a public forum. Though the show lasted only two short seasons, it made TV history. It was a media event so outrageous and so widely discussed it nearly rivaled the Watergate hearings.

Mary Hartman, the center of attention among her

from the script

AT COACH FEDDER'S MEMORIAL SERVICES IN MARY HARTMAN'S LIVING ROOM*

MARY: *Thank you, Reverend Buryfield, for that lovely introduction. And good morning, relatives, mourners, and ex-athletes. Although I never knew Coach Leroy that well on a personal basis, I certainly never meant to kill him. I only meant to be kind. He was sick, I made him some soup, he drank it, and by some act of God he then drowned. It is frightening to think that a little act of kindness could turn into a little mistake like that. A big mistake in Leroy and Blanche Fedder's life, of course—but a little mistake in the grand scheme of things. And now for my final point: I do not want any of my friends or neighbors ever to eat anything I offer them again. Even if I beg you. No! Please! If you come over, we'll eat out—or order in.* [THEN GLANCING HEAVENWARD] *Dear Leroy, wherever you are, know that I will think of you often—especially at mealtimes.* [SHE CURTSIES AND SITS DOWN]

Episode #43, Act I, VTR Date 2/5/76

Fernwood neighbors, gained her reputation for her preoccupation with "waxy yellow buildup." When a newspaper reporter arrived on her doorstep to find out her reactions to a mass murder in the neighborhood, Mary appealed to him to dispel her nagging doubt. "You've never been here before; do you see any waxy-yellow buildup on that floor?"

Mary's husband, Tom, was a former high school athlete and a working-class guy whose life began falling down around his ears when he made the mistake of running for a union position at his plant. Tom planned to fight corruption and got canned in-

Tom and Mary Hartman.

stead. He took to drinking, became an alcoholic, and all through the first season of the show viewers watched his slow and resolute slide into the gutter.

Tom's downfall could also be dated from the time he got involved with Mae, a voluptuous payroll secretary at the plant. Not knowing about Mae, Mary puzzled over Tom's new lack of sexual interest. She went to the library and took out a stack of books on "sexual dysfunction." When Mary came across a *New York* magazine article that described the theory of "the sexual diamond" (that men's interest peaks early and women's later), she brought her new discovery home to Tom.

"What the hell do you want?" Tom screamed when Mary broached the subject of their dormant sex life. "When we got married you said all you needed was me. Okay, you got me. Then you wanted a home, a house of your own. Well, I got *that* for you. Then you wanted to have a baby. Okay, I took care of that too. And I saw to it that you got a lot more. Just look at this kitchen. You've got a garbage disposal, a washer-dryer combination, a four-slice toaster, a radar oven. About the only thing you don't have is a trash compactor, and you know it's just a matter of time. So *now* what do you want???!!!" Mary, speaking in that thin, doll-like whine of a voice, answered, "I don't know, Tom. I want something. Something more. . . ."

Later, Mary's lanky, distracted, rejected, and octogenarian grandfather, Grandpa Larkin, showed up. Grandpa had achieved Fernwood fame by exposing himself at a luau for graduating nurses. "Do you have a minute for us to talk?" Mary asked him. "Mary," Grandpa answered, "all I have left are minutes." Mary asks him to tell her about life. "All right," he says, taking her at her word. "Life is like a three-ring circus . . . I might just as well have said life is like a hero sandwich. . . . There's only two things I can tell you, Mary. First, I love you." Mary begins to cry and Grandpa is indignant. "If I can't tell my own granddaughter I love her without her starting to bawl, I'm just going to have to leave it in a note after I'm gone." And then he tells her what happiness is: "Happiness is—like the kids say—it's finding out the thing you do best and doing it, doing it. As long as life allows you to, you do your thing. You don't have to do it great, you just have to keep trying. That's happiness." Mary wants to know how she should know what "her thing" is and Grandpa sighs. "That's the clinker in the deal. Nothing comes easy. . . ."

Mary and Tom Hartman had a daughter named Heather, whose fascination with platform shoes reached six-inch heights and who moaned about her lack of "bazooms."

Mary had to share her lover, Sgt. Dennis Foley of the Fernwood police, with her younger sister, Cathy, a meal-brained teenager who went through boyfriends like Fritos. Cathy specialized in defrocking priests and romancing deaf-mute poets.

The Hartmans' loyal best friends and neighbors were Loretta and Charlie Haggers. After launching her career as a country and western singer in the Fernwood Bowling Alley and producing such hit songs as "How Can You Say You Love Me When You Can't Even Talk Back?" to commemorate Cathy's love affair with the deaf-mute, Charlie and Loretta set off for Nashville to peddle a demo tape of her songs. Their car crashed into a station wagon carrying five nuns, the demo tape was destroyed, and Loretta was paralyzed from the legs down, an affliction which led her into the arms of Jimmy Joe Jeeters, a child guru with a sleazy father who later blossomed into Fernwood's mayor.

When Mary finally succumbed to the tireless entreaties of Sgt. Foley, they got together in the hospital bed where he was recovering from a heart attack. Once Dennis had her, he no longer wanted her. Meanwhile, Tom was settling down into a steady alcoholic stupor, the flight pattern from Fernwood's

Loretta Haggers (Mary Kay Place), *Mary Hartman's neighbor and best friend, country-western singer, and child bride of generous Charlie Haggers.*

airport had been rerouted to fly jets directly over the Hartman home, and Mary was dejected at failing in her effort to try to help her gay neighbor revive his "latent heterosexuality." Everything, including the sewage system in the Hartmans' front yard, was in a state of collapse. Mary went off to New York to have a nervous breakdown on David Susskind's TV show.

These were the lives of the people of Fernwood. Within months of going on the air *Mary Hartman, Mary Hartman* was quickly establishing itself as the media event of the decade. Not only was it undercutting Nielsen ratings of such pillars of the television kingdom as *Tonight* and the Chicago late-night news, but in San Diego, where it ran in a daytime slot opposite *Search for Tomorrow, Mary Hartman* was getting 49 percent of the share.

Charlie Haggers (Graham Jarvis), *Loretta's devoted, ill-fated husband.*

People either loved the show or hated it. In Richmond, Virginia, mothers protested and it was taken off the air. In Des Moines they got it pushed back from three-thirty to two-thirty so it wouldn't be on when the kids came home from school. Some thought it a mockery of American life; others thought it was the country's savior. Fans in Dayton, Ohio, held weekly meetings of "The Mary Hartman Tacky Fan Club." And a University of California extension course was offered—"Mary Hartman and the Rest of Us—A Nervous Journey into Televisionland."

The Mary Hartman phenomenon gave journalists a heyday. Louise Lasser/Mary Hartman was on the cover of major magazines from *Time* to *Rolling Stone* and *Soap Opera Digest*. And the soap opera magazines went nuts. This was an invasion of territory. Was *Mary Hartman* a soap or wasn't it a soap? Was it making fun of the genre or was it innocent?

Bryna Laub, editor of *Daytime Serial Newsletter*, denounced the show. *Mary Hartman* was "not only insulting to the intelligence of the soap opera audience," she wrote, "but also to those television viewers who have not had the opportunity to become familiar with daytime drama and are led to believe that this one-dimensional weak parody is in any way equivalent to the daytime productions. . . ." Meanwhile, Barbara Michels, editor of competitor magazine *Soap Opera Review*, wrote, "Comedy is Finally Here! In Norman Lear's production *Mary Hartman, Mary Hartman*, he has made space enough for us to step back and laugh. And then he pulls the rug out from under us so fast it hurts. Cliches and stereotypes turn out to be real. There is compassion and tenderness in an abandoned Chinese laundry [where Mary was held hostage by a mass murderer]. A mass murderer is a lonely boy, and Mary dries his tears. Paper doll characters suddenly bend. . . . They play it straight as comedy should be played. There's Mary Hartman. She smokes, she sighs, she mumbles, but she's not afraid to reach out and touch those close to her. . . ." John Leonard of *The New York Times* called *Mary Hartman, Mary Hartman* "the American interior monologue," and he suggested that you don't so much watch it as "paddle across it in a canoe."

Mary Hartman, Mary Hartman was the only nationally broadcast soap opera not seen on one of the three major networks. Instead it was sold to independent stations by T.A.T. Communications

from the script

MARY AND GRANDPA LARKIN ARE AT
THE KITCHEN TABLE:

GRANDPA: *This is the best cup of coffee I've had in years.*

MARY: *Yeah, me too.*

GRANDPA: *I learned to make it when I was in the army. Mary, I wish you could spend a couple of years in the army—it would give you a nice break from Tom and Heather.*

MARY: *Maybe there's a way I could get a break from Tom and Heather and not be in the army.*

GRANDPA: *You could* tell *Tom and Heather you were going to join the army—pack your duffle—and come stay next door with us.*

MARY: *I don't know if I could lie like that.*

GRANDPA: *Mary, you're a beautiful little girl and I want you to be happy, but it isn't always easy, is it? We know that, you and I. You expect more and I expect less, but that's just age. Of all of them, you're most like your Grandpa. You don't really belong here, do you?*

MARY: *What? I don't understand.*

GRANDPA: *That's the point, little Mary Shumway—there ain't nothing to understand. You know exactly what I'm talking about, you just don't want to admit it to yourself.* [HE GETS UP AND GOES TO THE DOOR.] *I think I'll go for my daily constitutional. It suddenly got boring here.*

MARY: *Grandpa—don't tell anyone, Ma or anyone, about this talk. It's very personal to me.*

GRANDPA: *Mary, I probably won't be around that long. It makes me a very trustworthy person.*

Episode #46, Act I, VTR Date 2/10/76

*Mary and Tom Hartman
face off over breakfast.*

Company, Norman Lear's independent company that does a host of highly successful situation comedies like *Good Times* and *All in the Family*. With no network involved there's no middleman, no "program practices" representative ready at every turn to stop the production to negotiate two "damns" for one "hell," and no commandment to change storylines or characters to push up ratings. Sidestepping the networks this way looked like a Norman Lear coup d'etat, but the truth was that it happened by accident.

Lear had wanted to do something in the soap opera form for years. He hadn't watched daytime soaps, but he did like the idea of an unending storyline. "It's the difference between a painting on a canvas and a mural on a full wall," Lear explained.

Al Burton, who has since become T.A.T.'s creative supervisor, worked on the idea for *Mary Hartman* with Lear from the beginning. "Norman's idea was to have blue-collar families and women with curlers in their hair and not looking the way the beautifully coifed women in soap operas looked," he recalled. Lear also rejected the idea of having all the people be middle-class professionals. He ordered a "split-level soap," a show that would play on two levels. On one level, viewers were expected to care for the people exactly as they would have if they were watching a regulation soap opera. On another, they could find a hilarious side to it. "Norman's vision was that it would be four-thirty in the afternoon, for example, and a businessman might pick up his telephone and call a friend to say, 'I don't know what this is on CBS or ABC right now, but you've got to tune in to it. It's funny.'"

Lear and Burton got together with comedy writer Gail Parent of *Sheila Levine is Dead and Living in New York* fame, and the three put together the plan for the comedy soap. They came across an article in *Life* Magazine about the dehumanized life of a worker on an assembly line in Lordstown, Ohio, and decided that would be their locale. "We figured we'd simply put a tract of homes there," Burton ex-

from the script

MARY'S KITCHEN—EARLY MORNING

[IT'S ABOUT FIVE O'CLOCK IN THE MORNING. MARY'S WEARING A ROBE OVER HER NIGHTGOWN, DEEP IN UNHAPPY THOUGHT, SITTING AT THE TABLE WITH TOM, ALSO IN HIS PAJAMAS UNDER A BATHROBE.]

MARY: *Tom, do you know it's going to be twenty-three years before our sexual desires are synchronized again?*

TOM: *What the hell is that supposed to mean?*

MARY: *I was reading an article. . . .*

TOM: [QUIET DISPAIR AT THAT DANGER SIGNAL]: Oh, boy . . .

MARY: *About the rise and fall of sexual desires between men and women. Did you know that it's like a diamond?*

TOM: [UTTERLY AT SEA]: *What??*

MARY: [PUTTING HER THUMBS AND FOREFINGERS TOGETHER TO FORM A DIAMOND]: *See, this here is the top of the diamond. Now, when men and women are in the embyro, their sex is practically the same. As a matter of fact, for a while you can't even tell if it's going to be a boy or a girl.*

TOM: *Yeah, so?*

MARY: *But then the baby is born and it's either a boy or a girl. And if it's a boy, his sexual appetite grows very quickly, much faster than a girl's, and when the boy is eighteen years old, he's right over here . . .* [KEEPING ONE HALF OF THE DIAMOND STEADY, SHE USES THE OTHER FOREFINGER TO POINT] *. . . on the diamond, at the very height of his sexual abilities.*

TOM: *Wait a minute. Are you saying I've been going downhill sexually since the age of eighteen?*

MARY: *That's exactly right. You've gone straight downhill.* [SHE POINTS AGAIN ALONG THE DIAMOND]

TOM: *What about girls?*

MARY: *Well, you see here's this* other *side of the diamond.*

TOM: *Never mind the diamond! What about a woman's sexual abilities?*

MARY: *You can't understand it without the diamond.* [DEMONSTRATES WITH THE OTHER THUMB AND FOREFINGER] *A woman's sexual desires and ability to perform develop much more slowly. Actually, she doesn't hit her peak till she's forty.*

TOM: [SHAKEN]: *Which means you won't be hitting your peak for several years yet—while I've been on the skids sexually for seventeen years. Right?*

MARY: *Right! I think that's right.*

TOM: *Great!*

MARY: *But don't worry.*

TOM: *Don't worry???*

MARY: *See—after forty, my sexual desires will decline very rapidly. So by the time we're sixty, we'll be completely synchronized again sexually—neither of us will want to have sex and everything will be all right.*

TOM: [NOT AT ALL REASSURED): *When we're sixty??*

Episode #46, Act I, VTR Date 2/10/76

plained, ''and the father would work in the plant and the husband would work in the plant and the next-door neighbor would work in the plant. If the plant went on strike, they'd all be out of work; if they're all laid off because of the economy, then we'd deal with the economy.'' Lordstown was later renamed Fernwood, the name of the street that runs behind the Lear offices in Hollywood.

During one of their planning meetings Gail Parent offered a title for the show—''The Life and Times of Mary Hartman.'' Lear thought a moment. ''You know what I see,'' he said. ''I see her mother two doors down, leaning out the window as she has all her life to call her, and her mother just says, 'Mary Hartman, Mary Hartman.' Let's call it that. Let's call it *Mary Hartman, Mary Hartman.*''

When Parent had to leave the project, they went in search of a new writer. By then Lear had figured out how he wanted to start the story: ''Mary's grandfather is found to be the Fernwood Flasher, there's a mass murder on the cul-de-sac right next to their street where five people, two goats, and eight chickens are killed, and there's a strike about to be called at the plant. . . .'' Each new writer they interviewed was confronted with what came to be known as ''the famous paragraph.'' One after another they laughed

At home, in their lumpy bed, Mary Hartman shows her husband, Tom, the New York *magazine article she has found that propounds a "Sexual Diamond Theory," that men's sexual appetite peaks before that of women.*

and said, "Yes, but seriously. . . ." Ann Marcus, who had done five years as head writer on two daytime soaps—*Search for Tomorrow* and *Love is a Many Splendored Thing*—and has since become head writer on *Days of Our Lives,* was the first to listen to the "paragraph," nod, and go right on telling the story. She got the job and brought on Jerry Adelman and Daniel Gregory Browne to help her. Together they began writing the scripts that were subsequently considered and turned down by all the major networks. "We think it's terribly funny, but our viewers won't get it," was the response at one network.

Finally CBS put up $100,000 to help finance two pilots, but when the pilots were done they decided not to go any further. At last, determined not to let their new show die, Lear and Burton decided to take the show directly to local station owners and managers. Lear flew twenty-three of them from all over the country to his home in Los Angeles. He served them dinner in his backyard and put *Mary Hartman* up for sale.

Shortly before the lawn sale, Al Burton had been speaking at a conference of academicians and TV critics in Aspen, Colorado. He had brought the two *Mary Hartman* pilots with him. "These academicians were a rather gimlet-eyed bunch, but I figured, what the heck. I gave a speech and told them they'd have to commit themselves to watching the whole hour." After the screening Ben Stein, then TV critic for the *Wall Street Journal,* came up to Burton and asked permission to review the pilots in his paper. It wasn't standard practice to review a show not on the air, but Burton agreed. The morning after Stein's review Lear got calls from *Time, TV Guide, Christian Science Monitor,* and the *Washington Post* asking why they had never heard of the show.

The review, entitled "A Dandy Show You May

from the script

MARY: *How do people know when they're enjoying themselves—I mean—during sex?*

LORETTA: *Lord, Mary, with all them flashing lights and crashing waves and skyrockets taking off, who wouldn't know they're enjoying themselves?*

MARY: [TENTATIVELY]: *Skyrockets? Is it really skyrockets?*

LORETTA: *It's skyrockets plus. It's like a train going through a long dark tunnel. Then suddenly there's a light and pow!! The train whistle starts screeching and that long, long train starts plunging out into the light with that crazy engine with the whistle blowing. It's like four minutes of skyrockets!!!*

MARY: *Four minutes?*

MARTHA [MARY'S MOTHER]: *I wish everybody would let me know what you're talking about. I've seen plenty of trains and Fourths of Julys—but what are you talking about?*

Episode #46, Act IV, VTR Date 2/10/76

MARY [GOES TO THE PHONE AND DIALS 411]: *Hello, information, I'd like the number for a Mary Hartman in Fernwood. H as in heart . . . art. M as in man . . . m-a-n. You don't? Do you have a Tom Hartman same spelling—you do? Do you have a Mrs.? . . . Mrs. Tom Hartman? . . . No? Thank you very much. I'm not listed.* [HANGS UP]

Episode #46, Act III, VTR Date 2/10/76

Never Get to See," is now hanging in Al Burton's office as a full-sized wall poster. ". . . the show is a scream," Stein wrote. "It is more sophisticated than Monty Python without the slightest pretention. It is more subtle than *Mary Tyler Moore* and just as funny. . . . Into the desert of game shows and soap operas, which are one millimeter from being parodies of themselves, *Mary Hartman, Mary Hartman* would introduce extremely fine comedy and a high degree of viewer involvement—if it gets

on the air. So far Lear is having trouble getting into the world of daytime programming with *Mary Hartman, Mary Hartman.* According to a Lear spokesman, unnamed network executives say they love the show but think it's too sophisticated for general audiences."

Stories praising the unaired soap opera appeared in major newspapers and magazines just as the station managers were arriving for dinner on Norman Lear's lawn. They watched the pilots, listened to Lear's pitch, and as soon as Al Flanagan of Denver stood up to announce he would buy *Mary* for his seven stations, the waters parted and the other station managers were in line.

The show got its revenge on the networks. In the second season the networks came begging to buy it. Lear turned them down. In addition to feeling a loyalty to the local stations, Lear and his production staff had gotten used to their new freedom. "I don't have someone from the network calling me up eight, ten, twenty-two times a show," Lear explained. "I don't enervate myself with telephone calls with somebody saying, 'Well, can't she say X . . . do they have to do Y?'"

Norman Lear is a small, friendly, and optimistic man. His trademark is the golfer's hat he wears perpetually, perhaps to keep ideas from springing unheralded from his head. Everyone in "the Lear organization," as it's referred to by its members, from secretaries to actors to writers, is encouraged to contribute ideas. But Norman, as he's called by all, always has the final say. With the help of a telephone installed in his car, he keeps his fingers in everything that's going on under his auspices.

The favorite device around the Lear offices is the tape recorder that is a perennial presence in any meeting or conference. Recorded transcripts are typed and distributed to participants so that every idea with a germ of potential ends up recycled into the creative process. When the chicken soup episode sprang full-blown from Lear's imagination during a script conference, Al Burton accompanied Lear's pantomime of the action with a running commentary so it could be recorded on tape: ". . . and he's got his head on the table and he's pulling at his sweater from behind. He's trying to lift his head. . . ."

Scripts for *Mary Hartman* were prepared far enough in advance to allow everyone a chance to react and suggest changes. But this collaborative method sometimes led to hurt feelings and down-to-the-wire arguments. For example, in the first year of the show there was a dispute over the resolution of Mary's affair with Foley. Lear didn't want Mary to be unfaithful. After much debate, they compromised. Dennis and Mary would be allowed to get together, but Dennis would have a heart attack in the process. This validated the traditional soapy morality: transgressions take place, but they have got to get punished.

Ann Marcus, the writer who put together the first season's scripts of *Mary Hartman,* has an undaunted anarchic view of the world and proved a special talent for coming up with storylines that were both disarmingly ordinary and completely unorthodox. Though she was at that time a renegade from the traditional soap opera world, her legit soap background was probably one of the keys to the success of that first season on the air.

In the second season she was gone. Norman Lear dispensed with the idea of having a headwriter for *Mary Hartman*; it would all be done by committee. Within weeks it was clear from the new writers' scripts that something was going wrong. The ratings dropped, and when *The Village Voice* wrote a criticism of the new season, saying that the magic was no longer there, Lear wrote back to *The Voice* himself, agreeing with the criticisms and promising an upswing promptly. But even though new writers were brought on, the old zany *Mary Hartman* was gone. The show seemed to lose its serial quality and be more and more like a string of not-so-funny situation comedy episodes. When the demise of the show was announced, its loss was hardly noticed. The faithful and even fanatic viewers of the first season had simply not been persuaded to come back.

But plenty of new TV ground had been broken by that first year of the show. In addition to the accidental discovery of the benefits of dealing straight with the nation's TV station owners, Lear and company brought a spontaneity and rawness to the screen that hadn't been seen since the Sid Caesar days.

It was a risky business, working in this collaborative Learian way. There were endless decisions to make and remake and quite often personal feelings were involved. Viva Knight, the show's producer, described it. "*Mary Hartman* is not rigid, ever. We make changes all the way. We're constantly reacting to someone who has come up with a new idea. The director will say, okay, let's try it. We're constantly learning a new way to do something. It's like doing a live show from the old days."

This creative chaos was completely opposed to the traditional network effort at an elegant and perfectly clean video image. Where regulation soap opera producers are always keenly aware of catering to their audience, Lear's one commandment in producing *Mary Hartman* was always "Reach for the outrageous."

"*Mary Hartman* has rough edges, but the audience forgives us our mistakes," Al Burton explained while the show was still running. "We make errors on *Mary Hartman*. It's not slickly done. It's not perfectly put together. The problems of the day are sometimes evident even in the production of the show. It's not like the soap operas that come on with a gloss and romance and unreality that is perhaps pleasing to the housewife at a certain level, but not really reflecting what's actually going on in her mind."

At home in Fernwood with Mary Hartman there was always a stack of *Sunset* Magazines that must have been piled up from the very first issue that arrived as a wedding gift. The Formica kitchen counters featured a pastel-colored cookie jar, a dish tray stacked to the ceiling with drying dishes, and two gold-sprayed ceramic cats. In Mary and Tom's bedroom there was a framed photograph of daughter Heather. Mary's dressing table was covered with a blue and white polka dot slip cover, and their bed was small and sunk in the middle.

These unglamorous and awkward sets were part of the fact that despite a peculiarity of plots that would be very hard to match, there was more reality in *Mary Hartman, Mary Hartman* than there was anywhere else on television. The offbeat humor of the stories allowed them to veer sometimes painfully close to the truth about the way people live.

"Let's take the old man who becomes a flasher," said Al Burton. "Not for reasons that are sexually aberrant, but simply for lack of attention. I mean, here is a guy whose pleasures in life, or should I say choices, are going to the Safeway and watching them unload melons or playing checkers in the park. And going to the Safeway has more suspense to it because one of the melons might drop. That poor older gentleman simply has nothing to do, and what do we have him do? We have him go out in a raincoat and flash; at least it got him some attention. I'm not saying that all of us can relate personally to that incident, but the responses we had in the mail from older people were amazing. We didn't deal with the ex-scion of a wealthy family, returning from a board meeting with nothing to do. We dealt with a man who is more like everybody out there. The fact that we look at his problem through flashing is simply to make it enjoyable. When he was arrested for flashing and he wanted to give the mitigating circumstances in order to defend himself, he said, 'What do I have to do all day? I sit, I walk, sometimes I lean.' Well, when you're looking at a man who's eighty-two years old and he says, 'What do I have to do all day—,' that's not spoof, that's not satire, that's the truth."

P.S.: One last bit of gossip: Louise Lasser, or Mary Hartman, whichever it is, wore a wig as Mary Hartman. Those placid braids that crowned her head with unrelieved languidity were not her own at all. The wigs, of which there were a few, were expensive items, costing somewhere in the neighborhood of $750 apiece. And there were two varieties. The ones with straight hanging hair were for bedtime scenes; the ones with braids were to wear by day. Louise's own hair, so the word goes, was actually short and frizzy.

Index